Circled Life

Salmon of the Strait of Juan de Fuca

by

Susan McDougall

Susan McDougall
Sequim, Washington
www.treeslivehere.com

Contents

Acknowledgements

Introduction 1

Oncorhynchus gorbuscha — Pink 11

Oncorhynchus nerka — Sockeye 27

Oncorhynchus keta — Chum 47

Oncorhynchus clarkii — Cutthroat 65

Oncorhynchus tshawytscha — Chinook 79

Oncorhynchus kisutch — Coho 97

Oncorhynchus mykiss — Steelhead 115

Acknowledgments

Information on the return of the salmon to the Elwha River since the final dismantling of the two dams on the river was enthusiastically shared by fisheries personnel of the Lower Elwha Klallam Tribe. Robert Blankenship provided an excellent, informative tour of the House of Salmon hatchery.

Data and insight into salmon dynamics in the eastern part of the Strait were provided by several employees at the Washington Department of Fish and Wildlife.

Kylie Stoneburner gave unceasing support for my volunteer work in counting returning spawners and departing smolts. Cheri Scalf took the photo of me in the salmon trap on Salmon Creek.

David Biek and Paul Dixon contributed to editing the seven essays included in the book.

The dedication of the North Olympic Salmon Coalition (NOSC) staff and volunteers has unfailingly provided personal inspiration and hope for salmon restoration. I have learned much from field work opportunities (such as tree planting) and educational forays into the field.

Introduction

Fifty million years ago a primitive, freshwater-dwelling salmon plied the waters of southern British Columbia and northern Washington state. This species differed from today's salmon by fine details such as teeth and facial structure, but its legacy is evident today with fish that range in size from the five-foot Chinook to the 20-inch Pink. As members of a modern genus — Oncorhynchus — these fish live in fresh and saltwater habitats at different stages of their lives. Oncorhynchus means "hooked snout," referring to the large, curved mouth (also called the kype) developed by breeding males, a modification that promotes aggressive behavior during the spawning season.

Most abundant in the cold waters of the northern Pacific, Oncorhynchus includes 16 species that range from Japan and Russia to North America as far south as Mexico and to the west. Seven species reside in the Strait of Juan de Fuca.

Of these, three are known as "trout," but all are members of the Oncorhynchus genus and share a lifestyle that includes birth and spawning in freshwater, and a saltwater residency during their years of maturation. Two species have forms that spend their entire lives in freshwater: these are the Kokanee, a lake dwelling Sockeye Salmon (Oncorhynchus nerka), and the Rainbow Trout, a small version of the Steelhead (Oncorhynchus mykiss).

Five species are anadromous, meaning they die after spawning. The other two — the Cutthroat and the Steelhead — can survive spawning and return to their natal stream in subsequent years or even forgo the arduous trip altogether. These are iteroparous fish, a word derived from Latin meaning "to repeat," and "to beget."

Dying after spawning implies a short lifespan and for most salmon species this is the case. The largest — the Chinook — on average matures in saltwater over a period of three years before returning to its birthplace, while the short-lived Pink is on a two-year cycle. Repeat spawners, such as the Cutthroat, can live as long as 10 years, although most often less. The hefty Chum mature at 3-5 years with a maximum lifespan of seven.

Except for freshwater forms such as the Kokanee, natural origin and hatchery salmon alike depend on the bounty of the productive cold seas and are intolerant of warm water. Many migrate to northern regions such as coastal Alaska, while others stay closer to home, seeking food in relatively shallow waters although sometimes foraging to depths of a thousand feet or more. Some travel far upriver to spawn, while others, such as the Chum, complete their life's mission in the lower reaches of their natal stream.

In the past, the seven salmon species plied the waters of the northern Pacific in vast numbers, sometimes turning the rivers nearly black with their closely packed bodies. All were answering an ancient call to return home. Forced southward during the Pleistocene Ice Age, their presence in the Strait following glacial melting most likely did not go unnoticed. Humans made new homes in a landscape now repopulated with the return of many plants and animals formerly excluded by the deep ice. What people thought as they established villages along coastal and riverine waters is unknown, but what is evident was the richly diverse culture that developed. It was a bountiful life, made possible by the dependable upriver migration of the salmon each year. And although this annual return sustained the people, it was not assumed that such benevolence was guaranteed. Ceremony and visual art, stories and observation — all acknowledged the importance of the fish to the people's well-being.

In time, these great numbers of salmon would be consigned to memory as new human settlers put pressure on the bountiful resource. It must have seemed too good to be true, all those fish! Now the "resource" would provide food for an expanding market, both domestic and worldwide. Fish were no longer consigned to the local table; they were food for distant peoples who knew little of their lives.

Fishing proceeded at a pace that might not have been

predicted but resulted in a freefall of salmon populations that in hindsight can be considered inevitable. As the search for new sources proved unsuccessful, the idea of enhanced reproduction, in retrospect, seems an unavoidable reality. Now hatchery-bred salmon would be released to the ancient waters of their wild-born forbearers. Unfortunately, the supplemented runs did not halt the decline of those fish born in the gravelly beds of a natal stream.

Yet it was not fishing alone that pressured salmon populations. Consequences of habitat alterations that accompanied expanding human populations implied spawning site degradation, while increased pollution, changes in stream and river courses, among other impacts, accelerated the decline. Even in the absence of fishing, the loss of clean waters and beneficial habitat meant fewer numbers of mature salmon.

As the collapse of stocks continued, efforts such as listing under the Endangered Species Act (ESA), enacted by Congress in 1973, at the very least put into place new requirements and restrictions as well as a call for both conservation and restoration, a directive that would be answered with a variety of programs. All were intended to meet the goal of increasing natural origin salmon numbers to the point of sustainability. This goal would prove to be very difficult to achieve.

Listing under the ESA required increased monitoring and less fishing — although not necessarily a halt — and a host of other responses to the difficult task of restoring what had been lost. Any progress brought hope, and publications that ranged from simple identification guides to scientific papers and books contributed to awareness, knowledge, and engagement.

Today, complex fishing rules reflect the requirement to increase salmon populations while supporting recreational, commercial, and tribal fishing. Legislation can open new monetary resources while organizations committed to salmon restoration engage in a variety of activities. Pressure on the land is addressed, sometimes through new regulations, other times by purchase and easements. It is a complicated arena in which any positive events, such as a good annual run of adults or juveniles is welcomed with a combination of relief and smiles.

The focus of this book is on the seven *Oncorhynchus* species that spawn in the rivers, lakes, and streams of the northern Olympic Peninsula. This includes the larger rivers that terminate in the Strait, such as the Dungeness and Elwha, as well as streams — Salmon, Snow, Jimmycomelately, and others. Hatchery-bred fish are released from several state and tribal hatcheries near the Strait.

Meanwhile, populations Chum, Chinook, and Steelhead have been listed as "threatened" under the ESA. For these, recovery plans are in place and both juvenile and adult fish are monitored at various levels. Fishing rules include restricted harvesting of listed groups. Coho, Pink, Sockeye, and Cutthroat are not listed in the Strait although the unique sockeye population at Lake Ozette, located near the northern outer coast, is considered threatened.

The seven salmon species are discussed in separate essays, each opening with an introduction that offers a personal perspective. This is followed by a discussion of a species' physical characteristics, such as size, weight, and coloration; also presented are the range and life cycle of the fish. A brief evolutionary background offers insights into geologically deep time, and Ice Age dynamics as well. Essays also delve into fishing issues, particularly where populations have been severely impacted; these discussions also examine other factors that have contributed to the decline of all salmon. Restoration and conservation are introduced; their importance to hope for the future is given particular emphasis.

A pastel painting of the species adds a visual element to each essay.

Introduction

Each species has unique characteristics that are encapsulated in this introduction with a simple phrase. It is my hope that the seven essays will offer a foundation for an understanding of these amazing fish.

The Species

Pink Salmon (*Oncorhynchus gorbuscha*) — "Too Much of a Good Thing"

This is a species that has in recent years increased rapidly in the Strait. It spawns on a reliable two-year (odd) cycle which makes it a favorite for hatcheries. Expanded hatchery releases with smolts numbering in the billions have raised concerns about the impact of Pink Salmon on the oceanic food chain, a dynamic, ever-changing pyramid that includes salmon and many other species as well.

Chum Salmon (*Oncorhynchus keta*) — "Local Restoration"

The Chum Salmon of the eastern Strait are part of the Hood Canal cohort, listed as a threatened Evolutionarily Significant Unit (ESU.) As such, the fish of the Strait have been the object of intensive restoration efforts, including supplementation in streams where the Chum was extirpated. Numbers have risen, offering a positive outcome and hope for other restoration projects.

Coho (*Oncorhynchus kisutch*) — "Data and Models"

Although not listed under the ESA in the Strait, the Coho is another species that has been on the brink. In 2017, the population was so low that by law a recovery plan was prepared and implemented. Available data for the Strait Coho is processed utilizing FRAM (Fishery Regulatory Assessment Model), a mathematical approach that incorporates estimated errors, stock abundance, and exploitation rate, among other factors. This model is used as a predictor for Coho escapement; that is, the number of fish that return from the ocean to their birthplace.

Steelhead (*Oncorhynchus mykiss*) — "Adaptation: the Fresh and the Salty"

An ocean-run fish that can spawn multiple times, the Steelhead is also present in a freshwater form, the Rainbow Trout. This is a popular sport fish, heavily stocked in lakes and streams. The saltwater form — Steelhead — is known to travel far offshore and is also a popular game fish. Along the Strait declining populations have prompted a petition to list all Steelhead from Salt Creek on the peninsula to the offshore waters south as far as Willapa Bay.

Sockeye (*Oncorhynchus nerka*) — "Two Ice Age forms"

The Sockeye Salmon includes a sea-run, anadromous form, and a freshwater, smaller fish, known as the kokanee. This fish is thought to have evolved more than once from the saltwater sockeye. Known for their bright red and green spawning colors, fish in the Strait are part of the Fraser River population, a run that at one time numbered in the millions.

Chinook (*Oncorhynchus tshawytscha*) — "Culturally Significant"

Also known as the King, the largest of the mighty Chinook was called the "Tyee," a fish that could attain a weight of 30 pounds or more. Rare today, the Tyee is representative of a species considered by some to be the most imperiled of all salmon. In the past, for many Indigenous people along the coast it was the greatest provider of all, with an importance manifested in art and story.

Cutthroat (*Oncorhynchus clarkii*)— "Versatility"

The smallest of all salmon species and known as a "trout," this little fish is unpredictable in its habitat preferences. Of the many subspecies that reflect this complex behavior, one occurs in the Strait. This is an iteroparous fish that sometimes forgoes spawning altogether. It may also choose to avoid saltwater forays as well, or occasionally linger in estuaries, perhaps to take advantage of prey abundance. Many populations are land-locked, while the coastal form is more free-ranging!

The Strait

From its rivers to its spits, to bluffs of glacial debris, the topography and composition of the many landforms represented in the Strait of Juan de Fuca is evident no matter which direction you turn. Rivers tell a story of ancient meanderings, while tumbling, eroding soils and rocks augment gravelly beaches. Occasionally a fossil emerges, washed clean by rain, having made its way to the surface of an eroding bank. It is a glacial landscape with evidence ranging from pebbles in streams to the deep Strait itself, a hundred-mile-long body of water where the intrusion of saltwater a few thousand years ago was most likely witnessed by watching and waiting humans. This new extension would provide a pathway to more southerly extensions, such as Hood Canal and Puget Sound.

The saltwater that followed the glacial melting would in time (sometimes very quickly in geological terms) provide a conduit for a host of species, from the smallest diatom to the mighty whales, nourished by each other in the cold sea. Following the icy retreat, salmon forayed into the Strait from the northern Pacific, perhaps in time via more southerly inland waters; here they would benefit from the nutritious cold waters. The subsequent increase in their numbers implied more food for birds, mammals, and yes, even plants.

Research indicates that the Strait was subjected to at least four glacial advances, the most recent being the Vashon Stade of the Fraser Glaciation and evidence from this event is found throughout the Salish Sea. Beginning over 20,000 years ago, the ice lobe extended into the Puget Sound and Strait basins, pushing westward to the Pacific via a low elevation conduit bounded by the Olympic Mountains to the south and the mountain ranges of Vancouver Island on the north. The ice crept upward to the base of the mountains, meeting extensive alpine glaciers that altered ancient riverbeds.

Glacial retreat has been variously dated, but recent evidence points to a maximum glaciation about 14,500 years ago. With melting, incursion of saltwater into the Strait and eventually the rest of the Salish quickly followed. In its wake, in the Strait the ice left a basin over 600 feet deep at its maximum with an average depth of 300 feet (100 m).

Although it is not known when humans first settled along the present coastline, opportunities for hunting Ice Age mammals indicate a mobility that could have facilitated entry to recently deglaciated lands. In time the largest mammals would disappear, even as the salmon returned to an ancient landscape, modified by an icy incursion that with its retreat offered unprecedented opportunities. The Strait was fresh territory for both the salmon and the humans who came to rely upon them. Rivers released from their frozen beds were not lifeless for long: the salmon had found an ideal place for their young. So, too, had the people who partook of the bounty offered by the salmon's return.

Introduction

Today, despite the many factors that have impacted salmon populations, the people and the salmon remain bound together through an ancient connection. Acknowledging cultural memory of their abundance, today, hope for the salmon rests in the actions of many, often representing widely ranging interests, but all committed to the preservation of these iconic fish.

Circled Life

Oncorhynchus gorbuscha - **Pink**

Nearing the end of its journey to a calm sea, the river seemed to quicken as it flowed in great arcs of white-and-green torrents over boulder-strewn rapids. The water pulsed with unreleased energy, tearing at the banks and rolling gravel and stones along the river's bed, an ancient physical force that few mortals could challenge. And yet, if you looked closely, across the undulating surface thousands of little fins punctuated the torrent. These were the fins of the smallest of all salmon — the Pinks. Black from above, sometimes flashing a reddish-green accent, or the tip of a snout, the two-year-old fish were coming home to spawn.

A teenage boy reached into the cold water and grasped a fish. Smiling, the lad held the fish briefly, then returned the creature to the river and watched as it joined its companions. With strength and determination, each pushed against the flow, responding to a call that humans could never fully understand.

The smallest but most abundant of the Salish Sea salmon, the Pink Salmon's common name refers to its spawning colors. Silvery-blue on the back and pale on the belly during its ocean residency, as the mature fish returns to freshwater, it is transformed to warm pinks and cool greens. Also called the "Humpback," the descriptive name refers to the male's rounded back, a modification acquired as it enters estuaries during its autumn spawning run. The male also develops a hooked mouth (the genus name *Oncorhynchus* means "hooked snout"), sometimes so enlarged that he cannot close his jaws.

Aside from the male's hump during spawning season, this species is most easily recognized by the large, black, oval spots along the back and sides above the lateral line, and on both lobes of the caudal fin. Adults can reach 30 inches (76 cm) in length and weigh as much as 14 pounds, but more typically on average they are 20 inches (51 cm) long, and approximately 8 pounds.

Most common in the north Pacific, the Pink Salmon inhabits waters as far west as the Lena River in Siberia and east to the

Mackenzie River in northern Canada. Along the west coast of North America, this species ranges south to La Jolla in southern California where it is uncommon.

Pinks have been introduced to many seas throughout the Northern Hemisphere, as well as in freshwater bodies, such as the American Great Lakes. They are present in the White Sea and Barents Sea of northern Europe and have established populations in the north Atlantic as far west as Newfoundland. In Norway, increased numbers and an expanded range have made the Pink Salmon a "high risk" species, particularly for its impact on the native Atlantic Salmon (*Salmo salar*.)

***Oncorhynchus gorbuscha* - Pink Salmon**

From Washington to Alaska along the Pacific coast, Pink Salmon is the most numerous salmon species. In Puget Sound alone approximately 3.7 million were estimated to have returned to local rivers in 2021, with little evidence of any future decrease. As a regular spawning salmon in the Strait of Juan de Fuca's largest rivers, numbers exceeding 300,000 were projected that year, a substantial increase over previous runs.

However, these large numbers are not an annual phenomenon, as Pink Salmon hatch, mature, and spawn in a two-year cycle. For most of the eastern Pacific, the majority return to freshwater in odd-numbered years.

Typically traveling a short distance upriver, the female Pink searches for suitable gravels in which to deposit her eggs. Finding an acceptable substrate, she turns onto her side and scoops out a redd (a depression) with her body and tail. In this "nest" she will lay as many as 2,200 eggs. Watched carefully by males, following fertilization the female begins another excavation upstream, pushing gravel over the eggs just laid.

Females may live as long as 20 days after spawning. Hatching occurs in 4-9 months, and the young emerge from their protective cover at about an inch in length. They do not linger but rather are soon carried downstream. Entering the estuary, the juveniles move swiftly to saltwater where they seek the protection of shallow eelgrass beds or migrate seaward as much as 30 miles (50 km). At sea, most of their lives will be spent in relatively shallow waters — 33 ft (10 m) or so — although they will occasionally descend to as much as 243 feet (74 m) below the surface.

With a preference for cold waters, Pinks consume a variety of invertebrates and small fish and grow rapidly in their oceanic habitat. Sometimes known to migrate far offshore, they have been observed in streams 400 miles (640 km) from their birthplace.

After their migration to the sea, Pink Salmon remain for only a year-and-a half, maturing quickly over a single winter before embarking on their journey back to freshwater. This brief residency accounts for the two-year cycle of the species; it is the shortest for any salmon. In the Strait, their return to the Dungeness River is divided into an upper river population (early) and a larger lower (late) one. To the west, the genetically distinct remnant Pink population in the Elwha, formerly confined to the river below the Elwha Dam, has recently increased to the low thousands, as today the adults travel farther upriver, spawning in tributaries, such as the Little River, and the main channel alike.

Hatchery Supplementation — the Dungeness and the Elwha

Although Pink Salmon are the most numerous of all salmon species, healthy runs coupled with rapid declines in the Salish Sea compounded concern over their status during the past 50 to 60 years. These numbers tell a story only partly understood but disturbing in its implications, not only for Pink Salmon but other salmon species as well. In 1963, the return of at least 100,000 (and possibly more) spawning adults in the Dungeness River was recorded as a high point for the species. It was followed by a long, persistent decrease, one attributed to habitat threats.

In the Elwha River, the presence of two large dams had suppressed Pink Salmon numbers for 80 years, keeping the species on the brink of extirpation in the river. Meanwhile, the free fall on the Dungeness continued, with fewer than 3,000 spawners recorded in 1981; twelve years later the returning fish numbered less than 2,000. Subsequent returns in the following years included a particularly alarming decline in 2003, attributed to a severe flood on the Dungeness in 2002.

These consistently low numbers in the early years of the 21st century were addressed by a request for supplementation with hatchery-produced fish. One available facility for such a proposal was located on Hurd Creek, a tributary to the Dungeness River.

With operations beginning in 1980, the Hurd Creek hatchery is located approximately three miles from the mouth of the Dungeness. Constructed for the purpose of enhancing salmon runs in response to alarmingly low numbers, hatchery programs at Hurd Creek have historically been in place for the well-known Chinook Salmon as well as Steelhead, Coho, and Chum.

Oncorhynchus gorbuscha - Pink

Augmentation of the Dungeness Pink Salmon population began in the first decade of the 21st century and has continued to the present.

Pink Salmon eggs at Hurd Creek are collected from odd-year Dungeness River spawning natural origin fish. Such an autumn collection and subsequent juvenile production is regulated by agencies responsible for hatchery programs. Released the spring after hatching (even-numbered years) the number of these first-year fish reached a maximum of over 100,000 in both 2010 and 2012. Releases have declined in more recent years in response to river conditions and saltwater survival rates for both maturing juveniles and migrating adults. Such dynamics in the numbers of adult salmon complicate predictions of both young and mature salmon alike.

Located farther up the river, with historicl release numbers varying from approximately 50,000 in 1957, to over 1,350,000 in 1969, the Dungeness River hatchery has been a site of Pink Salmon augmentation for more than a hundred years. With broodstock originating in Finch Creek, a Dungeness River tributary, juveniles were released at Hurd Creek.

Return to the Elwha

Effectively blocked by dams on the Elwha River for most of the 20th century, salmon species that had spawned in the river since prehistoric times declined to mere shadows of their former numbers. Completed in 1913, the smaller 108-foot Elwha Dam was located approximately 4.9 miles (7.9 km) from the river mouth. By 1927, construction on the Glines Canyon dam was finished. Twice the height of the Elwha Dam, this dam was licensed for hydroelectric power generation while the lower Elwha Dam was not.

Prior to dam construction, the Pink Salmon population was estimated at between 400,000 and 600,000 adults. And although

the number was significantly reduced, thousands were
nevertheless observed below the Elwha Dam in the 1950s and
1960s. However, a bulldozing project designed to improve flood
control contributed to a rapid Pink decline, and when the Lower
Elwha Klallam Tribe fisheries' personnel began surveys in the
1990s, spawning adults had been absent for several years.

In the largest dam removal project ever undertaken in the
United States, in 2012 demolition of the Elwha Dam on the lower
river was complete, and two years later Glines Canyon Dam was
taken down, thus removing the final barrier to the emptying of
Lake Mills above the blockage. With the Elwha flowing free once
again, hope increased for the return of natural origin salmon.
However, the impact of increased sediment during dam removal
raised the specter of Pink Salmon extirpation. This concern
prompted the collection of Elwha Pinks for supplementation.
Spawned at the Hurd Creek Hatchery and reared to adults at the
NOAA Manchester Research Station, in total, intervention took
place with three brood cycles —2011, 2013, and 2015 — of the
river's Pinks.

As part of the Elwha salmon recovery efforts, in 2011 the
Lower Elwha Klallam Tribe (LEKT) House of Salmon hatchery
began operation. The goal was to raise Chinook, Coho, and
Steelhead for the purpose of augmenting runs and to improve
ecosystems in and along the river. At that time, wild salmon
spawning activity for all species had been primarily confined to
sites below the Elwha Dam. But, except for the collection during
dam removal, undertaken to preserve nearly extinct runs, Pink
Salmon was not included in the House of Salmon hatchery
program. Nevertheless, in the second decade of the 21st century,
as people watched and counted, a steady if fluctuating return of
adult Pinks did begin.

Encouraging as the sightings were, only in the last two
spawning cycles (2021, 2023) did the numbers indicate that the
Pink Salmon might be viable in the Elwha. And these returning

spawners are genetically distinct from nearby populations, including those of the Dungeness River, another positive sign for recovery.

In 2023, as many as 5,000 spawning Pink Salmon entered the main Elwha River channel and tributaries as well. There is hope that the Pink Salmon have returned.

Dungeness Pinks

The Dungeness Pinks consist of two runs, an early spawning event from July to September in the upper river, and an autumn one beginning in September in the lower. Returning Pink numbers have varied widely, from a high recorded in 1963 sinking to the low thousands in 1981, in the wake of a severe flood. The impact of such an event, which although uncommon is not unprecedented, offers some indication of the fragility of this most abundant salmon. Recovery in the Dungeness was so slow following the flood that by 1987 the count had fallen to 138. This extremely low number motivated the request for hatchery production of Pink Salmon.

A slow but oscillating climb began in the first decade of the 21st century with the augmented count reaching 125,000 by 2013 and then declining sharply once again. With spawners numbering in the low thousands in 2017, perhaps because of a warming event in the north Pacific — the so-called "blob" — in 2023, the Dungeness River Pink Salmon stock had rebounded to approximately 150,000. The reason for this maximum is not clear although it is conjectured that two good La Niña years were a factor.

Today, bridges over the Dungeness offer opportunities to witness the large Pink runs of recent years. Yet throughout the Salish Sea and north to the icy Arctic, augmented by hatchery production, some have come to question the possible impact of such high numbers on other species, including salmon.

Circled Life

Pinks — Millions to Billions

In the past, Pink Salmon spawning adults numbered in the millions. Even on the Elwha, where all salmon species went into free fall following dam construction in the early 20th century, the Pinks may have numbered more than a million. And it was not just the Elwha that supported so many. Throughout the Salish Sea, Pinks blackened the water in autumn with their anxious bodies, each striving to reach their birthplace in the many rivers that emptied into the sea. They traveled up the Columbia River, spawned in California streams, and from Korea to Siberia thrived in the cold rivers of east Asia. In the mighty Fraser River alone, it is estimated that in the early 20th century, prior to a rockslide in 1914 that interfered with passage upriver, the Pinks numbered nearly 48 million.

With its two-year life cycle and rapid growth rate, Pink Salmon are clearly a very fecund species, one expected to consistently reappear in odd-numbered years. And for thousands of years, this uninterrupted and undisturbed small salmon did just that. While other salmon species suffered severe loss, the Pinks held on.

Or so it seemed. Today, researching Pink Salmon numbers, both in the past and in 21st century updates, introduces yet another worrisome story of species' decline. And the Pinks have not been left out of the picture. A species that once provided sustenance for those who depended on the sea and the rivers, now numbered in the thousands rather than the millions. It was a clear call to action, and one to be addressed by society's simplest answer — build a hatchery.

And if you were planning and implementing hatchery production, economically the Pinks were the best salmon species to consider. The two-year cycle meant release could occur in a single spring season. And, regular as a clock, a year-and-a-half later fully mature adults, fattened in the productive sea, would be back. Or at least some of them. Meanwhile, in the open sea near their hatchery homes, the prolific Pinks would support a robust fishery.

The numbers of hatchery salmon are huge. In 2022 alone, 40 million Alaskan hatchery-produced salmon were commercially harvested, a number that rivals ancient runs. That year, fisheries' personnel collected 2.1 billion salmon eggs and released 1.9 billion juvenile salmon.

Wild Salmon Decline — The Hatchery Fix — Alaska

In 2022, approximately 23 million hatchery-bred Pink Salmon returned to Prince William Sound, located in Southeast Alaska. This is a region where hatchery salmon outnumber natural origin salmon; it is estimated that at least 76% in the Sound are hatchery fish. The goal, however, has never been to replace natural origin salmon, although inbreeding is a concern where the numerical balance is so heavily tilted towards hatchery fish.

Historically, Prince William Sound was considered a relatively pristine environment, a place where wild runs were not excessively impacted by habitat loss. How, then, did the Sound become home to so many millions of hatchery-bred Pinks?

In coastal Alaska serious hatchery augmentation of salmon began in the 1970s; here, commercial harvest in the early years of the decade was a fraction of the highs experienced 40 years before. Worried about the state's fishing economy, Alaska's constitution was amended to permit hatchery construction. The idea was not to replace natural origin fish, but to add to their numbers, to create "healthy, well-managed wild production." Hatchery fish could be harvested, in part paying for hatchery costs and hopefully taking pressure off the declining wild populations.

Today, there are 30 hatcheries in the state, most operated by private nonprofit corporations (PNPs), and since the late 1970s growth, while not constant, has increased the commercial salmon harvest to much greater numbers than ever recorded. The natural origin salmon take has accelerated as well, reflecting in part the recovery following the Pink's decline. Commercial take of hatchery salmon has been up-and-down, with a high point in 2013.

The numbers reveal the story, but there is so much data to absorb that at times the overall picture of natural origin and hatchery salmon throughout the North Pacific is obscured. Salmon production in Asia as well as North America contributes to population counts so large that you might wonder why alarm calls over hatchery contributions to the robust numbers are made at all. Even the worry over hatchery "strays" inbreeding with natural origin populations seems less troubling.

A perusal of some of those numbers is worthwhile nonetheless, as it offers insight into the role hatcheries play in the north Pacific today. Most importantly, with such a rebound, it is important to ask what society intends for the future of the iconic Pink Salmon.

Big numbers do stand out, and one of the most instructive is fish biomass in the north Pacific. From 1990-2015 it was estimated that 48% of the total for three salmon species — the Pink, Chum, and Sockeye — was contributed by Pink Salmon. This number exceeded five-and-a-half million tons, with 40% of adult and immature salmon biomass attributed to hatchery production, a number that increased from 0.9 billion juveniles to 5.1 billion between 1970 and 1990. It is estimated that 15% of the Pink Salmon numbers from 1990 to 2014 were hatchery fish, the majority released in Alaska. During that time, natural origin Pinks were also at a high point, with approximately 60% originating in Asia. Today, 3 out of 4 salmon in the north Pacific are believed to be Pink Salmon.

In the North Pacific, favorable conditions beginning in 1977 led to increases in natural origin and hatchery fish alike, to the point that competition for food at sea may have reduced growth and survival rates and negatively impacted other salmon species; this shift also affected predators such as seabirds and mammals. These concerns are prompting research into the question of species' dynamics, particularly given the changes wrought by the warming oceans.

South of Alaska

Habitat degradation, overharvest, and other negative consequences of human activities have impacted all salmon species along the coast and the inland waters of the Pacific Northwest. Yet the Pinks seem to have turned the corner from the sharp decline of the latter 20th century, with an estimated 3.9 million reported in 2021 in Puget Sound alone. However, the number does not translate directly to size; in general, the average Pink Salmon weight has been decreasing for several decades. And, as with the concern in Alaska, the question of when an apparently good outcome (an increase in numbers) becomes a less desirable one (pressure on resources) is difficult to answer. In the past, the waters of the Salish Sea and the Pacific Ocean supported fish so numerous that it is difficult to visualize such richness, but the reality of reduction to the point of Endangered Species Act (ESA) listing, as well as concern over so many salmon populations is one that must be considered when evaluating impacts. Such is the case with the Pinks.

Pink Numbers — Too Many Fish?

From 2005 to 2021, Pink Salmon runs in the north Pacific Ocean, a region which encompasses waters from Russia and Japan across the Bering Sea to southeast Alaska, British Columbia, and Washington, reached their historic high: it is estimated that this species now represents 70% of all Pacific salmon.

Circled Life

On average, odd-year spawners outnumber even by a factor of twenty-five. This difference can serve as a "control" and provides an opportunity for researchers to evaluate possible impacts of Pink Salmon on other species. While investigating prey, such as zooplankton, squid, and fish, studies also consider air-breathing fauna, including seabirds and mammals. And although fluctuations in prey abundance undoubtedly occurred in the past, the cyclical nature of Pink Salmon numbers has provided researchers with evidence of this species' impact on the food web. It is the extent of correlations between Pink Salmon abundance and other species, particularly the phytoplankton upon which zooplankton feed, which is revealed.

This relationship between Pink Salmon and prey is not always straightforward, and impacts can be positive, negative, and cyclical in nature. As an example, when zooplankton decreases because of heavy predation from Pinks, phytoplankton, now subject to less browsing, increases. Studies also reveal that in years when Pink Salmon numbers were reduced, zooplankton increased.

Species such as herring, perch, and squid are especially subject to predation by maturing Pink Salmon. The fluctuation in squid alone is particularly notable, as they are an important prey for other salmon species, as well as birds and mammals, and are considered a vital part of the marine food web.

It can be argued that ups-and-downs have always been part of oceanic system dynamics. The concern is over numbers. What happens when balance is lost between species dependent on similar resources?

The implications of Pink Salmon numbers are evident in more subtle ways. As an example, prey consumption by other salmon species points to a Pink influence. Chinook and Sockeye salmon consume less nutritious prey during odd-numbered years, when

Oncorhynchus gorbuscha - Pink

Pink Salmon growth rate is at a maximum. Timing of entry from river to sea is also important. As they migrate from freshwater to saltwater Pink Salmon juveniles consume prey in common with other smolts, such as those of Sockeye and Chum. Competition with Chum Salmon at sea continues during odd years when maturing Pink Salmon are especially abundant, resulting in reduced prey, typically of less caloric value.

Potential side effects of the abundance of Pink Salmon, including the annual input of millions of hatchery fish, are considered by many researchers to mediate the carrying capacity of the north Pacific Ocean. Such modifications to a system are referred to as a "top-down" effect, particularly pronounced when a species' abundance undergoes large-scale changes. It implies an interaction with other species that may be indirect; for example, the swings in zooplankton abundance that occur in response to the Pink Salmon odd-year spawning cycle.

One of the least understood changes is the rise in sea temperatures brought on by increasing greenhouse gas concentrations in the atmosphere. Labeled today as "climate change," the reality now becomes more apparent each year, and the fallout goes beyond bigger storms and rising atmospheric temperatures. The sea, too, is changing.

Warming Seas and the Pinks

Aside from hatchery numbers, fluctuations in odd-year Pink Salmon spawning cycles, and the impact of such factors on other species, evidence that Pinks respond well to an increase in sea surface temperatures adds to concerns about the oceanic food web. It is generally acknowledged by researchers that in the late 1970s a so-called "regime shift" to warmer waters resulted in a cascade of effects on marine ecosystems. While many species declined, in the North Pacific Pink Salmon populations increased, in part due to hatchery production but also in response to sea temperature. On the Strait, the abrupt rise in Pink Salmon numbers in the Dungeness River may in part have been a response to the temperature increase.

While warming seas might have given Pinks a competitive edge, in general increased temperatures create more demands on the body, resulting in a greater need for high caloric food. Particularly of concern are larger species such as the Chinook, but all salmon species tend to decrease in size where this biennial competition with Pinks takes place. Additionally, large numbers of hatchery fish add to the demands on food supply. And smaller spawning size implies fewer juveniles — large females produce more eggs.

In the second decade of the 21st century, high temperatures coupled with increases in Pink Salmon populations (over 1.34 billion adults in a two-year period) in the North Pacific Ocean may have played a role in the precipitous decline of other salmon species, the largest recorded drop in history. In 2020, harvests declined in the double digits, reflecting suppressed numbers at sea; it is conjectured that such a free fall was not a result of Covid, where both fishing and surveys were reduced, but rather a decline in fish populations. It was a worrisome trend.

Enter the Blob — A Temperature Limit?

First detected in 2013, by the winter of 2014, a warming sea event off the southwestern Alaska coast had spread to encompass more than 2,000 miles (3,200 km) of eastern Pacific waters. Named the "Blob," this increase in temperature was unprecedented, at least in the history of record-keeping; in February of 2014, the water temperature was approximately 2.5° C (4.5° F) warmer than average. By 2015, the Blob had dissipated, but the impact remained. Warming in the coastal waters of Washington, and south as far as California, resulted in a loss of phytoplankton and the nutrient-rich zooplankton that eat them. These small creatures are critically important in the salmon diet.

If the observed decline in Pink Salmon numbers is an indication, this abundant species was apparently among those affected by the Blob, with sharp declines in juveniles as well as adults. The impact was present for more than one spawning odd-year cycle, as reduced size alone implied fewer eggs; additionally, a local drought may have contributed to the decline. The Blob affected Pink Salmon throughout the North Pacific, resulting in a 2017 "federal disaster" being declared in the Gulf of Alaska for the Pink fishery. The bailout cost the government over $56 million.

Apparently, even the Pink Salmon has tolerance limits to increased temperature. Perhaps the primary cause is a decline in nutritious prey — the decrease in "crunchies" as opposed to the increase of "squishies," as one commentator notes. Yet in 2023, the numbers seemed secure, the fisheries increased their catch, and the outlook was positive. Other forces, such as prices, will continue to play their role, but today the Pinks are very numerous.

In The Strait – Loss and Return

It is hard to grasp an increase of more than 145,000 spawning Pinks in 10 years, but that is the case in the Dungeness River. The slow increase began from a low point of fewer than 2,000 in 1987 to current numbers. However, fluctuations in returns have been consistently worrisome and in the 1990s petitions were filed under the auspices of the ESA for listing two populations — the lower Dungeness River, and the Elwha. Accepting a recommendation by the National Marine Fisheries Service, this petition was denied, the reason given that Dungeness Pinks were part of a larger and healthy Evolutionary Significant Unit (ESU).

Meanwhile, from a handful of Pinks in the Elwha during the 1980s to numbers in the low thousands, a continuing increase is an encouraging sign for the river, and certainly a different outcome for what once was considered an extirpated population.

But the biggest concern over Pink Salmon in the North Pacific is that there are too many, a scenario that affects many species and is exacerbated by unprecedented hatchery releases, particularly in Alaska. Increased competition for food manifests itself in a cascading effect. From orcas to seabirds to other salmon species, the worry over "too many Pinks" will most likely increase as the ocean continues to warm and recurring heat wave events add to the pressure on all creatures, from the tiniest plankton to the multiple-ton whales, all dependent on the sea.

From millions to thousands and back again. What does this mean for salmon, mammals, birds, and the many other creatures of the oceans as well?

It is difficult to conceive of the numbers of Pink Salmon that thrived in the northern Pacific Ocean prior to changes in the modern era that included large-scale fishing, habitat degradation, and warming waters. If, as some researchers have advocated, the Pinks are more tolerant of increased temperatures, is it possible that this species will dominate on an even larger scale than today? Or will, at some point, the Pacific Ocean waters be too warm to support a food supply adequate even for the Pinks?

The halcyon days of millions of Pink Salmon turning the rivers into a living mass are over. The immediate future for the species seems secure, at least for those born in hatcheries. Perhaps the changes brought on by a warming world imply a future for the oceans' species that are beyond the human ability to intervene, and although it may require commitment and compromise not easily achieved, I remain hopeful that a balance is possible.

Oncorhynchus nerka - Sockeye

From the tiniest sculpin to the platter-like sunfish to the dogfish shark, for someone who is fond of fish, almost any sighting will do. Yet it is always best to keep expectations in check, as these ancient creatures can vanish as quickly as they appear. Theirs is a watery, viscous world, one that molds and sustains them. For air-breathing creatures, excursions into their realm are brief, and for most observers, the featureless waters are only viewed from above.

So, when you walk across a lakeside parking lot, looking for flora rather than fauna along its edges, and just happen to come to a small but vigorous stream that flows into a deep, stunningly blue lake, and flashes of deep red break the surface and stir the waters, then, from a fish encounter point of view, you know it is a really good day. For here,

Sockeye Salmon, the kokanee form in a crystal-clear stream

only a few feet away the creek provides a temporary home for Kokanee, the landlocked freshwater form of an otherwise quite conventional salmon.

The place was Lake Chelan, located deep in the dry mountains of central Washington. Two hundred miles to the west, the Kokanee's saltwater relative had begun its own transit through the cold waters of the Strait of Juan de Fuca, bound for a deep and swift river north of an international border of which the salmon was unaware. All that mattered was a keen sense of the direction to its natal home, where, hungry and spent, it would give all it had left to the next generation, and rest at last.

Circled Life

A fish with two names that reflect distinct although linked lifestyles, the Sockeye (*Oncorhynchus nerka*) is an ancient species with a genetic fluidity that enabled adaptation to Ice Age dynamics. One form, named the sockeye, is typically anadromous, spawning in streams and lakes and maturing in the sea, while the other — the kokanee — is strictly a freshwater fish. In particular, the kokanee lives in lakes, sometimes completely landlocked and isolated by physical forces such as climate change and geologic events. Stranded, the kokanee shares a common ancestor with the sockeye, and both are most likely descended from a saltwaters progenitor.

"Sockeye" does not refer to the eyes, but rather is a Salish name. "Kokanee" means "red fish," from the deep, warm color of the flesh. Anadromous sockeye are larger than the kokanee, but nevertheless rank as the second smallest salmon, greater in size than the Pink Salmon (*Oncorhynchus gorbuscha*) but much smaller than the three-foot Chinook (*O. tshawystcha*). The sockeye stretches to a maximum of 33 inches and a weight of 15.5 pounds, although the typical length is less than two feet and 3.5-8 pounds. By comparison, the kokanee is most often 8-15 inches long, an indicator of a freshwater rather than a richer marine diet.

Both forms of the Sockeye (the capitalized word refers to both the sea-run sockeye and kokaneel) lack black spots as adults, although spawners can show some dark markings. The head is large, and the mouth lining is black. At sea, the sockeye is bluish green above with silvery sides and white below. Spawning sockeye are bright green to olive on the head with a contrasting red body; females tend to develop paler shades of red and green. As they approach their spawning grounds, males are most easily distinguished from females by their dorsal hump and hooked jaws lined with prominent teeth. As they mature to spawning age, the kokanee also transform from silvery-blue to reddish hues.

The sockeye is the most range-limited of all salmon. A northern fish, they are distributed from Japan, across the Pacific to

Oncorhynchus nerka - Sockeye

Kotzebue Sound near the Arctic Circle, and along the Pacific coast to southern California, although they are rare south of the Columbia River.

Widely introduced in lakes throughout the United States, the kokanee is sought by anglers from Washington to Maine and along the Pacific coast. In the Southern Hemisphere, sockeye eggs were imported to New Zealand as early as 1902; populations there are landlocked, with most in decline. Sockeye have also been introduced in Patagonia.

Artificially spawned in hatcheries, the more numerous

Oncorhynchus nerka - Sockeye Salmon

anadromous sockeye is also stocked in rivers and streams, particularly in Alaska. In the Northwest, the largest natural origin sockeye runs once numbered in the millions in Canada's Fraser River. This population is the most common sockeye in the Strait of Juan de Fuca; during spawning season they transit from southwest to northeast. Sockeye also return to the Fraser via Johnston Strait, east of Vancouver Island.

Circled Life

Sockeye hatch in about 2-6 months following fertilization, emerging at night. The fry mature in lakes for 1-3 years, although most depart by their second year. They remain in nearshore waters and migrate during fall and winter; typical residency in saltwater is two winters. They are known to move northward far offshore, often reaching Asian waters. Most spawning occurs in summer and fall, but returns can range across several months. Runs are typically earlier in the north, but in large freshwater rivers such as the Fraser, spawning occurs from summer to late fall. It is not uncommon for the offspring of several populations to be present in the same lake.

A cold-water species, sea-run sockeye can tolerate temperatures as high as 59° F (15°C) but prefer waters that range from 37-48°F (2.5-9°C). Kokanee like slightly warmer conditions, but both do best in cool waters. This makes the species particularly vulnerable to ocean warming, a consequence of climate change.

Most maturing anadromous sockeye forage in water depths from the surface to 44 feet (10 m) or less. Sockeye females produce 2,000-5,000 eggs, depositing them in several nests over a period of 3-5 days; fertilization often involves more than one male. Although the typical spawning age is three years, some adults live as long as 8 years. Kokanee females lay from 200 – 1,800 eggs; their redd (nest) is sometimes located in deep lake water.

Anadromous and lake-dwelling fish may spawn at the same time in streams and rivers, and hybridization is known to occur between the two forms.

In their rearing lakes, sockeye and kokanee fry feed on invertebrates. At sea, the maturing sockeye consume a variety of prey, including zooplankton, small fish, and squid. In turn, they are sought by a variety of predators, such as other salmon and sharks, as well as seabirds, seals, and whales. For human consumers, this is primarily a sport fish that nevertheless supports a commercial fishery throughout much of its range. In

Alaska, hatchery fish augment the sockeye take, while in the Fraser River most are natural origin fish, unusual in the world of salmon fishing.

Evolution

Fifty million years ago, an ancient Sockeye relative occupied freshwater habitats in northeast Washington state and southern British Columbia. This was *Eosalmo driftwoodensis*, the oldest known member of the Salmoninae, a subfamily of the Salmonidae family, to which all *Oncorhynchus* species belong. At the time, much of the region was subtropical, although upland lakes provided cooler waters for many fish, including this extinct species.

In the early Miocene Epoch (15-20 million years ago), the Salmoninae split into the northern Pacific *Oncorhynchus* and the *Salmo* genus, primarily an Old-World group of approximately 50 species, represented along the east coast of North America by the Atlantic Salmon (*Salmo salar*). Fast-forward another 10 million years or so, and the *Oncorhynchus* species recognizable today had separated into 16 northern Pacific species, with the divergence of the Pink and the Sockeye occurring most recently: this event may have been in response to topographical changes along the Pacific Rim region. It is also noteworthy that modern salmon species evolved before the onset of the Pleistocene Ice Age approximately 2.6 million years ago: it was apparently not the icy cloak that precipitated salmon diversification.

With the onset of the Pleistocene, Sockeye, as with other salmon, would have been confined to glacial refugia, most likely the so-called "Beringia" region, located in the northern Pacific, and "Cascadia," including the Columbia River, and other more southerly rivers. Today, two major genetic groups, one that ranges from Kamchatca to northwestern British Columbia, and the other located south from the Fraser to the Columbia, are considered representative forms of these glacial refugia.

It is possible that the kokanee arose several times from sea-run sockeye, most likely following deglaciation approximately 15,000 years ago. The derivation of kokanee from the larger sockeye is evident from the observation that kokanee populations are located within anadromous sockeye distributions and have not naturally dispersed beyond those boundaries. Research indicates that there were separate origins in different watersheds, giving rise to multiple colonizing events.

At least two questions come to mind when considering the evolution of the Sockeye. Given that new habitats became available as deglaciation followed the most recent Pleistocene maximum, why is the Sockeye the only *Oncorhynchus* to have adapted to distinct lifestyles? Certainly, such opportunities must have been present for other species. Second, although sockeye can be strictly riverine, most anadromous sockeye are dependent on lakes for reproduction. Kokanee and sockeye spawning takes place in streams and rivers near outlet streams, and fry occupy lake habitats for one to three years, feeding and growing until they reach smolt size. When sufficiently mature, sockeye then migrate downstream to saltwater. Thus, the young of both forms are often present in the same area. Why is there not more inbreeding between the two, given the mixture that naturally occurs?

Although sea-run sockeye and kokanee are the same species, in time they may diverge sufficiently for separation; they are considered by some researchers to be "actively" evolving. Inbreeding does occur, but variable run timing, and strong site fidelity tends to suppress genetic mingling. And kokanee are sometimes completely isolated, often by migration barriers, preventing incursions into streams and rivers.

The development of the two Sockeye forms is certainly an intriguing occurrence in salmon evolution. As the ice melted Sockeye were poised to follow rivers and streams to newly formed glacial lakes, an unprecedented opportunity on both sides of the north Pacific. Separated by life choices, sometimes enforced by geological and biological events as well, the sea-run sockeye and the kokanee are still considered as one. It is an acknowledgement of a recent, blink-of-an-eye separation.

Across the ocean, however, at least one descendent, confined to a single lake in Japan, has been designated as a separate, if closely related species.

Sockeye in the Strait

Except for the Fraser River sea-run sockeye that passes through the Strait of Juan de Fuca, regional lakes that can support sockeye or kokanee are few. The terrain is steep, and most rivers flow rapidly from the mountains to the sea. Lake Sutherland is the only lake that discharges into the Elwha River, while Lake Crescent drains via the Lyre River directly to the Strait. However, a waterfall on the Lyre blocks migratory fish passage, thus preventing Sockeye from spawning in or near the lake. The Lake Crescent population is truly landlocked.

Both lakes support kokanee populations; origins of this smaller fish probably date to glacial retreat several thousand years ago. However, subsequent hatchery introductions have complicated the genetic mix of the Lake Crescent and the Lake Sutherland kokanee.

As the glaciers released their grip on land and sea, other dynamic forces altered the terrain. Approximately 7,000 years ago a landslide sliced an ancient lake that had drained to the Elwha via Indian Creek. Two lakes were created in this singular event, one eighty feet higher in elevation and much larger than the other. This was Lake Crescent, a 12 mile-long, deep body of crystal-clear water, now cut off from the Elwha River. The smaller lake — Sutherland — continued to drain to the ancient river.

With a maximum depth of over 600 feet, Lake Crescent is

home to endemic forms of Rainbow Trout (*Oncorhynchus mykiss*) and Cutthroat Trout (*O. clarkii*), with record-holding members of both species that hint at a food source other than invertebrates. Apparently, these large trout enjoy an excellent diet of resident kokanee!

Home to a kokanee population, the much smaller mile-long Lake Sutherland has a mean depth of 57 feet (17 m) and a maximum of 80 feet (24 m). Prior to construction of the Elwha dams in the early twentieth century, these kokanee may have shared habitat with an anadromous sockeye population that spawned in Indian Creek and resided in the lake for a year or two. In 1913, the completion of the Elwha Dam, located below the confluence of Indian Creek and the Elwha River, blocked sockeye access. At this time, the lake's kokanee became an essentially landlocked population (both dams on the river lacked fish ladders).

Yet, as with Lake Crescent, the background of Lake Sutherland kokanee is more complicated than the story of water access dynamics altered by natural forces, such as landslides, and human impacts, as with dams.

Between 1933 and 1964, approximately 7 million kokanee smolt were released into Lake Sutherland. These fish were sourced from four hatcheries, including one built on Barnes Creek, a stream that empties into Lake Crescent. Released to augment the population, primarily for recreational fishing, it seems likely that inbreeding between the resident kokanee, an isolated group that may have arisen thousands of years ago, and the introduced hatchery fish would occur. That the kokanee were present prior to hatchery augmentation has been confirmed from historic fishing accounts.

Today, ten years after the last dam removal, fisheries' managers hope for a return of Elwha River sockeye to Lake Sutherland or perhaps a reverse wandering of the lake's kokanee down Indian Creek.

Oncorhynchus nerka - Sockeye

However, one question about a potential saltwater incursion for the Lake Sutherland kokanee concerns its physiological ability to adjust to the difference in salt concentrations between lake and sea. At least one study that quantified the saltwater adaptability of kokanee, sockeye, and hybrids between the two, indicated that kokanee had a much smaller window for acceptable plasma sodium concentration, a measure of saltwater tolerance. For yearling saltwater sockeye, this number was considered sufficiently low beginning in late March, and extending through August, a reasonably large window for the migrating fish. By contrast, for kokanee the lowest plasma sodium level was delayed until the end of May and exhibited a steady increase after that time. The window was much smaller.

Both forms displayed the highest adaptability in midwinter, a response to smolt development. Although this transformation is common to both the sockeye and the kokanee, researchers have questioned the possible energetic cost to the kokanee, the idea being that in their freshwater habitat, smolting may be unnecessary. It has been conjectured that this cycle reflects the genetic legacy of sockeye, but studies of kokanee isolated since the last glacial maximum also show this ancient ability to regulate sodium.

Given the reduced window for kokanee saltwater adaptation, another question concerning its return to a freshwater/saltwater cycle is whether such an event, in a sense, is a "reverse" evolutionary course. Researchers agree that kokanee developed from anadromous sockeye, and most often they are considered the same species. And the tendency for Lake Sutherland kokanee to produce large eggs adds to the puzzle, hinting at a close connection with Elwha River sockeye before dam construction. Perhaps the Lake Sutherland kokanee will at some point move downstream to the Strait. It remains an intriguing unknown.

Lake Crescent kokanee also have a complicated history. Prior to the ancient landslide, sockeye access to the lake involved a transit up Indian Creek. Even if the slide preserved the sockeye run, fish in the lake would have been isolated by the subsequent rise in its level, and the impassable waterfall on the Lyre River, their only connection to saltwater after the slide.

Historically fished, with the construction of several state hatcheries in the early twentieth century, in Lake Crescent supplementation with hatchery kokanee began in 1913 and continued until 1939. And as with Lake Sutherland, genetic mixing of natural origin and hatchery fish undoubtedly occurred in Lake Crescent.

Following removal of the two dams on the Elwha it was hoped that Sockeye might return to Indian Creek and establish a spawning population near the outlet of Lake Sutherland. Expectations also included the possibility that the lake's kokanee, previously denied access to the Strait by the Elwha Dam, might follow the creek to the river and subsequently to the sea. Yet, more than ten years after dam removal, evidence of any new connections between the lake and the Elwha are absent.

In fact, studies of Elwha sockeye indicate that a small number in the lower river are came from freshwater sources as far north as Alaska, and, slightly closer, the west coast of Vancouver Island. Collected from 2010 to 2017, a period that included specimens both before and after dam removal, 45 adult sockeye were analyzed. This was made possible by use of a genetic database which provided the most plausible origin for the sampled fish.

All of the Elwha sockeye were determined to be strays from other riverine/lake locations. Important to the question of local origins, none were from Lake Sutherland. Nearly half sampled in 2015 were assigned to Vancouver Island, specifically to lakes that drain into Barkley Sound on the west side. Of the remaining 23, initially 15 were identified as most closely related to the Stikine River sockeye; this Alaskan River is more than 620 miles (1,000 km) from the Elwha.

Such a distant assignment brought into question the accuracy of the genetic database, in particular the probability that stock identification was incomplete for closer sources. After considering this possibly, researchers believed it was likely that half of the sampled fish were strays from nearby rivers, such as the Dungeness, or rivers that terminate along the Washington coast. Only one specimen was from the Fraser River, a result that implies little straying from those sockeye that traverse the Strait.

Since riverine sockeye are believed to wander more than the lake form, it seems possible that a sockeye run may in time become established in the Elwha. Whether a connection will be made between the resident Lake Sutherland kokanee and the river is unknown. Origins, habitat, physiological responses, including but not limited to the transition to saltwater, and the availability of prey, among other factors, are important to the question of a spawning population of Elwha River sockeye.

Meanwhile, in the Dungeness River an exceedingly small run (6 or so adults) of spawning sockeye provide support for the idea that this salmon can maintain a population with a minimal number.

The Case of the Large Eggs — a Closer Look at the Lake Sutherland Kokanee

Kokanee are considerably smaller than anadromous sockeye, averaging less than a foot in length compared to the two-foot sockeye. And, as expected, most female kokanee produce eggs much tinier than their cousins. There is, however, an exception, one that involves a population with a genetic history complicated by the mixtures of ancient, current, and hatchery fish. It turns out that female Lake Sutherland kokanee produce eggs of the same size as the anadromous, river-dwelling sockeye.

This tendency towards large eggs indicates a possible anadromous background for the Lake Sutherland kokanee, perhaps even prior to the landslide that separated the shallow lake from Lake Crescent. The population may have been modified by sockeye influx via Indian Creek. It is also possible that planted fish were not only kokanee but also included anadromous stock. Or perhaps the kokanee are descendants of a very ancient population. Such conjectures add to the mystery of the lake's fish.

Fishing the Sockeye and Its Landlocked Form

Commercial and recreational fishing of the Fraser River sockeye that pass through the Strait on their spawning run is not presently permitted south of the international border. The run itself is the largest natural occurrence in the northeast Pacific, historically consisting of millions of fish that, after migrating to Alaska, return to the Fraser along both sides of Vancouver Island. The number in the Strait during the survey of 2010-2017 was estimated at a yearly average of 1.88 million fish.

The size of the return depends on annual conditions both north of Vancouver Island, and within the migratory route to Alaska. Likey seeking the coldest waters, Fraser River salmon are known to undertake this long route northward. Their return route as well may depend on water temperatures.

Kokanee are not currently supplemented with hatchery fish along the Strait, but the Umbrella Creek hatchery at Lake Ozette contributes to the ESA-listed "threatened" stock there. And while the Fraser River sockeye is primarily a natural run, increased supplementation programs have been instituted for sockeye blocked access to their spawning sites by a landslide on the river in 2021.

On the Olympic Peninsula, Lake Sutherland provides an opportunity for anglers hoping to catch a kokanee. Open from April to the end of October, fishing is permitted prior to spawning: the kokanee population of the lake varies between an estimated 4,000-6,000, most of which spawn in November near the Falls Creek inlet.

Oncorhynchus nerka - Sockeye

As with other Salish Sea species, fishing for sockeye dates
back thousands of years, with indigenous fishers employing
methods later adapted by American settlers. Since the late 19th
century, the take increased, in part because fishing was linked
with cannery processing, an industry that during seasonal salmon
runs could produce thousands of cans each day. For the sockeye,
the fishery was particularly rich in the so-called "Salmon Banks,"
located on the Strait offshore from San Juan Island. In 1792,
Spanish explorers had commented on the seemingly limitless
sockeye numbers and other salmon species as well, and by the
end of the 19th century, native tribal fisheries had been essentially
supplanted by much larger operations as canneries popped up to
take advantage of the autumn Fraser River sockeye run
concentrated in the banks.

By 1934 the resource had declined to the extent that making
easy money had become hard.

Today, the Salmon Banks are occasionally fished, but sockeye
are no longer a commercial target within its shallow boundaries.
The rich industry has died, but the numbers taken during its
heyday give some indication of how numerous the sockeye really
were. For example, in the summer of 1900, on average nearly 2,000
fish were processed daily from July through August. This number
could vary widely; in 1917, a high of over 28,000 fish in one day
dropped to 134 two days later. Overall, in 1917, over 45,000
sockeye were trapped and processed in local canneries. Those
facilities provided work for many, including immigrants and local
people as well, and were places of frenetic activity during the
sockeye run.

As with other such concentrated fisheries, the Salmon Banks
sockeye bonanza could not last, and in this case a natural event
beyond human control contributed to the decline. While the
production of 450,000 cases of Sockeye in 1913 marked a high
point in the cannery industry, coincidentally, less than six months
later year a rockslide at Hell's Gate on the Fraser River blocked

access for spawning sockeye. A freefall in numbers, coupled with legislation that banned traps, effectively spelled the end of the Salmon Banks fishery.

After the Slide — Cooperation

The large population in the Strait is attributable to the migration dynamics of sockeye smolt that exit the Fraser River estuary by the millions each year. Originating high in the Canadian Rocky Mountains, the river is 854 miles (1,375 km) in length and drains nearly one quarter of British Columbia. Major tributaries add to the flow as the river passes through climatic zones that range from high mountains to dry interior regions to the salty waters of the Salish Sea. Home to seven salmon species, many lakes within the Fraser River watershed provide excellent spawning and rearing habitat. For management purposes four sockeye runs are recognized, ranging in timing from early summer to late fall.

Mitigation of the Hell's Gate rockslide that spelled the end of the Salmon Banks' fishery began within a month as rubble was removed and fish were transferred in nets over the blockage. Yet despite ongoing efforts to widen the river, salmon numbers plummeted. Prior to the rockslide, the Fraser River sockeye population averaged more than 10,000,000 annually, with high points of 40,000,000 fish estimated at the turn of the twentieth century. Following the slide the run fell to less than a million, with recovery numbers measured at less than half the former abundance, at least until the latter part of the 20th century. By that time, concrete "fishways" transported spawners around the slide, and in 1985 spawning channels were constructed. By 1990, recovery looked promising as sockeye numbers trended upward, at least for a time.

Although intervention could reduce the impact of slides such as the one that occurred at Hell's Gate, the natural fluctuations of sockeye populations coupled with the consequences of both increased fishing pressure and natural events, including climate fluctuations, would within a few years prompt a cooperative approach between Canada and the United States. Twenty-three years after the slide, the first sockeye management plan between the two countries was ratified: the purpose was to restore the Fraser River sockeye run. In 1985, a treaty designed to protect five salmon species was signed by the two countries. A regulatory body named the Pacific Salmon Commission (PSC) would oversee the treaty's implementation.

Reporting to the PSC on an annual basis, the Fraser River Panel (FRP) was formed in 1985 with the directive of managing the Fraser River sockeye and Pink salmon fisheries. Each year, panel members recommend a fishery allowance based upon statistical and modeling approaches to the Fraser River salmon populations. The panel is also responsible for developing preseason management plans. They are involved with details, not just broad generalities, including run size predictions, status reports, escapement goals, modeling results, and comparisons between forecast and return at the season's end.

The FRP meets several times throughout the season to evaluate the ongoing fishery.

New estimates of the four Fraser River runs are often followed by adjustments to the catch allotments for both countries. These efforts are an aid to evaluating both the accuracy of predictions and fishery impacts on the Fraser sockeye.

The numbers are large and so is the potential catch. Unfortunately, the forecast error can be large as well. In 2022, the pre-season forecast was 9,775,000 sockeye. Of this number, nearly 550,000 sockeye were allocated to the United States; 67.7% of this half-million was specified for Tribal Treaty fisheries. An upper limit of 2,172,000 was granted to Canadian fisheries. The final seasonal escapement estimate was 6,936,000 fish, in part because of the small numbers of two Fraser River runs. The return yielded

7,009,000 fish, the smallest since 1990 and less than three-quarters of the preseason prediction. The exploitation rate that year was 23 percent.

The run predictions of 2022 were not the only ones to miss the mark. In 2019, a run size of 4,795,000 fish was estimated; the final was 571,000 fish, the smallest since record keeping began. This number may have been a result of the warm water "blob" in the northeastern Pacific, but such a conjecture is considered by managers to be simplistic, given that the impact is not consistent across species. Whatever the cause, the numbers were exceedingly low yet followed a relatively good year of approximately 10,864,000 fish in 2018.

Given the difficulties in modeling the Fraser River runs, and the unknowns associated with issues such as climate change, the FRC carries a heavy responsibility. The future of the Fraser sockeye lies in large part on approach, mathematical accuracy, and response to concerns as well as environmental dynamics. Accurate predictions are hard to achieve, and securing the sockeye's future, one always subject to unknowns, has become more difficult in a world of warming oceans, and pressures from many sources.

The object of human legislation and worries, mature sockeye answer an internal demand to return to the Fraser, responding to external clues in complex ways barely understood. As smolts they had migrated north to Alaskan waters, where most of their lives were spent. Returning southward towards the tip of Vancouver Island, they continue along the coast of the island, with the majority following the coldest waters. For those fish that swim the open waters of the island's west coast a turn northeastward takes them through the Strait of Juan de Fuca for the first and last time. Exhausted, they enter the Fraser River's fresh waters, continuing upstream on to their birth home. There they will spawn and die.

Unfortunately, the news continues to be worrisome in the third decade of the 21st century, and another rockslide on the

Oncorhynchus nerka - Sockeye

Fraser only added to concerns. In part, the most recent decline in Fraser River sockeye has been attributed to the Big Bar Slide of 2018. Located 40 miles (64 km) north of Lillooet, BC, this landslide created a 49-foot (15 m) waterfall, blocking the upriver sockeye return. It is estimated that 63% of the total sockeye run must pass this site to reach their spawning grounds. Following the slide, mitigation processes such as transporting salmon with helicopters and enhancing the population with broodstock eggs were part of the approach to increasing sockeye runs. However, the outcome of the slide, coupled with other factors such as delayed snowmelt that led to excess water flow during the summer, further exacerbated the problem of spawning salmon; thus, many did not travel beyond the lower river.

In 2018, the catch was 3,699,400. In 2019, the year after the Big Bar slide, the number was 94,400 returning Fraser River sockeye.

While there are short timescale events (the Big Bar Slide) that can unleash a steep decline of salmon numbers, more long-term dynamics such as warming oceans, competition from hatchery fish, disease, increased predation, runoff timing, and other factors add to the difficulty of estimating populations. One certainty, however, is that the overall trend for the Fraser River sockeye has been downward, with low points in 2020 when the count was 291,000, the lowest recorded since record keeping began in 1893. During the 20th century and continuing into the 21st, highpoints of over 25,000,000, a rare maximum coupled with the freefall of 2016 characterize the broad swings in the sockeye population. Such numbers are a source of dismay to managers, commercial fishers, anglers, and the tribes alike. While the future of the Fraser River sockeye may in part rely on informed human endeavors, the unknowns are worrisome.

Circled Life

In 2024, the Fraser River sockeye forecast is approximately 567,000 returning fish. Acknowledging this low number, at a meeting on March 1, the Washington Department of Fish and Wildlife (WDFW) proposed closure of specific Marine Areas, including, among others, the east Juan de Fuca Strait (Area 6) and the San Juan Islands (Area 7) fisheries.

Listing the Sockeye

It is unfortunate that Lake Ozette, a lovely, isolated lake located within the boundaries of Olympic National Park near the coast, has been severely impacted by a decades-long logging industry. Prior to restrictions on streamside and lakeside tree removal, the impact on tributaries was significant, with sediment loads that muddied the gravel in streams and the lake as well. This factor alone contributed to lack of suitable habitat for salmon spawning; additionally, encroachment by vegetation led to the reduction of prime habitat. Further complicating the lake's status, sediments have increased, while the mercury level peaked in 1990 at one of the highest levels in the state. Nine years later the Lake Ozette sockeye Evolutionarily Significant Unit (ESU) was listed as Threatened under the Endangered Species Act.

At the time of the listing, the recovery goal for the Lake Ozette sockeye was set at 31,250-121,000 spawning fish. It was also noted that to reach such goals an increase of 1.02 to 1.03 percent per year would be necessary. Unfortunately, this goal has to date proved unreachable, as over the past four decades the numbers have ranged from 4,398 to 12,829, with measurable downturns reported in a five-year review, initiated in 2019.

A few hundred miles southeastward, in the desert-like landscape of Washington state, the Snake River sockeye struggle to maintain a viable population. Listed as Endangered under the ESA in 1991, in 2022 the National Marine Fisheries Service (NMFS) recommended retention of that status. The Snake River

Oncorhynchus nerka - Sockeye

run was historically decimated by dam construction, and surveys indicate little change. A five-year NOAA review in 2022 confirmed the natural origin sockeye low returns, which never topped 500 in the 21st century. This is a population augmented by hatchery salmon, increasing the number to approximately 1,500 at a maximum. The Snake River population remains at high risk of extinction.

Yet sockeye can apparently maintain runs of small numbers, and in the Strait, they benefit from restoration projects design for other species. The removal of the second Elwha dam in 2014, offered an unprecedented opportunity for the Olympic Peninsula Sockeye. And although the return has been low and the fish that enter the rivers are often strays from distant places, it can be hoped that sockeye native to the Elwha will increase and with time lead to a sustainable population.

Unlike humans, the sockeye is consistent in its behavior, returning to its natal stream or lake, only to sacrifice its life to a few thousand eggs. Bright red bodies deteriorate as starvation sets in, but theirs is a life of admirable determination. Physical objects may stop them, biological forces prey upon them, but the goal is never lost. They will always strive to reach their birthplace.

And what other salmon likes lakes, saltwater, and rivers alike? The ice of a million year's duration provided opportunity, while the sockeye offered flexibility.

As for me, I would like to see the bright red bodies and the grass-green heads of the spawning sockeye once again. Perhaps it would be in a small stream, or a lake where territory is precious in the shallow waters. It need not be large numbers, as the less-than-ten size of the Dungeness River spawners can attest. To witness the efforts of a returning wild fish, its dedication and destiny both inflexible and in some sense, quite pure, offers both instruction and inspiration. It is most welcome at a time when so much seems lost.

Visions of millions of sockeye dance in the mind, while hope for the future rests in humanity, with its mathematical models, its surveys, and its attempts to understand. All contribute to the goal of continued existence for the red salmon.

Oncorhynchus keta - Chum

I pulled my knee-high rubber boots over my lined rain pants, zipped up a theoretically rainproof jacket, and topped off the outfit with a wool hat and cotton gloves. Nearby, my companion waited, anticipating her first visit to Jimmycomelately Creek. Our instructor accompanied us, as net and bucket in hand we began a short walk to a fish trap, temporarily installed in the stream near a busy highway bridge.

As we came to a halt near the trap, I listened for sounds of life within the gurgling waters but heard none. We carefully followed instructions for removing the heavy wood cover which, when lifted, would reveal the dark bodies of salmon within the

enclosure. Our purpose was to net them quickly, determine their sex, count, and release them back to the creek.

The trap was empty. True, it was the first week of the survey, but nevertheless our disappointment replaced anticipation. We talked about procedure, looked downstream, and began the task of replacing the stout lid.

And then we saw it. A two-foot, heavy-bodied fish, fitted out in its beautiful spawning colors, accelerated into the trap, tail flexing rapidly from side-to-side. This was a Chum, coming home to spawn — and to die.

I felt like I had stepped into another world, a watery planet where creatures with strange forms and alien purpose dictated the terms of life and death, beneath the surface and above as well.

Circled Life

The surroundings seemed to recede as we focused on lifting the surprisingly heavy, wonderfully foreign fish. Yet a few million years into its evolutionary path, this shiny creature had entered uncertain waters, for now it was dependent on humans for survival. And ensuring the continuance of this vulnerable being was why we three humans stood at the water's edge.

Three weeks later my partner and I were rewarded with the presence of many fish in the trap. They didn't like us much, or maybe they simply wanted to continue as quickly as possible to their place of birth. But for me, the feeling of leaving one world and entering another never diminished. As we approached the stream each week, I listened for the sounds of restless bodies and once again anticipated an encounter with the incredible Chum.

Of the seven salmon species in the Salish Sea, the Chum Salmon is the second largest, with only the mighty Chinook (*Oncorhynchus tshawytscha*) exceeding it in length and weight. The genus name *Oncorhynchus* refers to the hooked upper jaw that the male develops as it returns from the ocean to the river where it was born. Weighing in at a maximum of 33 pounds and a length of 40 inches (102 cm) from the tip of the nose to the end of the tail, the Chum more typically ranges from 9.9-15 pounds and 22 inches (58 cm). It is fusiform in shape with an upper jaw that extends beyond the back of the eye. Said to be most easily distinguished by the blackish mouth cavity, in its sea-run form the Chum resembles other salmon species, with a dark metallic-blue back and silvery sides. Yet compared to its cousins, the Chum Salmon is almost spotless, with only a few faint black markings occasionally visible on its back.

During breeding season, when mature Chum begin their journey from the sea to freshwater, the fish is transformed so brilliantly that it is hardly recognizable as that silvery-blue fish of a former life. Now the adults take on a blackish-olive hue, with reddish-pink and gray vertical bars on the sides, rather like irregular tiger stripes. A kaleidoscope of color, the Chum is unique. At this time as well, the male develops the hooked jaws and elongated curved teeth typical of salmon. He is hefty and dense, while the female shows a more rounded belly, revealing the precious eggs she carries.

The Chum is a widely ranging species at home in the North

***Oncorhynchus keta* - Chum Salmon**

Pacific, with populations inhabiting cold waters as far west as the Lena River in Siberia, south to Japan and Korea, across the Pacific to Alaska's northern Beaufort Sea, east to the Mackinzie River, and south along the British Columbia coastline to warmer locations in central California. In Washington state, the Chum breeds in many rivers of the Salish Sea, including those of the Strait of Juan de Fuca, and the lower Columbia River as well.

Also known as the Dog Salmon, the name apparently refers to the utilization of the Chum for dog meat, as it was never considered the tastiest of salmon. Although it was important as a subsistence fish, the negative comments were plentiful, with the flesh described as "coarse," and "inferior." Thus, it is not surprising that the Chum fishery remained small, at least until the overfishing of other salmon redirected attention to this large species.

In the past Chum eggs had been harvested as caviar, but with the expansion to utilizing the whole fish, new names besides "Chum" and "Dog," were adopted for marketing this beautiful if tasteless salmon. One of the best is "Silverbrite" although it is not exactly clear what inspired this choice; perhaps it was the blue-and-silver color of the saltwater form.

Evolution and Life History

The origins of the salmon family (the Salmonidae) are dated to an event in which the genome doubled, a process known as "autotetraploidy." This alteration results in an organism with four sets of chromosomes rather than the typical two. Research indicates that the doubling occurred in the salmonids at least 60 to 100 million years ago. It is believed that tetraploidy may offer some advantages, such as providing a mechanism for rapid evolution: it may also increase some resistance to inbreeding. The change has persisted to the present, with the Salmonidae family itself believed to have arisen no later than 50.8 million years ago.

Approximately 20 million years ago *Oncorhynchus*, the genus to which all northern Pacific salmon belong, split from *Salmo*, a much larger group well-represented by Old World species: the Atlantic Salmon (*Salmo salar*) is the solitary species in North America. With separation, divergence began, and by 6 million years ago, the anadromous salmon of the Pacific Northwest had evolved into seven species — Chum, Pink, Chinook, Sockeye, Coho, Cutthroat, and Steelhead. Dating to 6-8 million years ago, their oldest known fossil relative is *Oncorhynchus ketaopsis*, a species that may have been a repeat spawner.

There are three spawning runs of Chum Salmon in the Salish

Oncorhynchus keta - Chum

Sea, a "summer-run" — a population which begins its landward journey in late August or early September and ends in mid-October — a "fall run," and the less common "winter-run" which occurs from December through January.

Most Chum Salmon spawn in the lower reaches of their natal rivers and streams. Large and heavy, the Chum lacks the jumping prowess of other salmon, such as the Coho, but possesses a powerfully strong body that can "muscle" its way over gravel covered by only a couple of inches of water. And some do travel far from their saltwater home; such is the case in the Yukon River, where spawning can take place 1,678 miles (2,700 km) from the river mouth.

With a maximum lifespan of seven years for the female Chum, most maturing fish remain in saltwater for 3-5 years where they consume a variety of invertebrates and fish. In turn, they are preyed upon by other fish such as Pacific halibut, sharks, and lampreys: seabirds, whales, and seals also find them tasty. At sea they are known to forage in waters as deep as 1,312 feet (400 m) but are most often present in shallow depths.

Like other salmon of the Strait, Chum Salmon inhabit cold water, although they do exhibit a relatively large temperature tolerance: during migrations temperatures as low as 32° F (0° C) with a maximum of 70° F (21.1° C) are sometimes endured. However, Chum typically spawn at temperatures from 44.6 —55 ° F (7°–12.8°C), with optimal conditions at around 45° F (7.2° C); young salmon are known to die at 53.6° F (12° C).

Upon reaching suitable spawning sites, female Chum Salmon dig a redd (nest) in clean gravels, scooping a depression and depositing as many as 3,500 eggs. They often lay more than once but also show a tendency for aggressiveness towards other fish: such disagreements may result in failure to spawn. Following fertilization by an attendant male the female covers the eggs. Their bodies totally spent, both sexes die after spawning, most often within a day.

Circled Life

After 1.5-6 months of incubation, fry emerge from the gravels and migrate directly downstream. They do not feed in freshwater, but will remain near the shoreline, often in brackish waters, where they take cover in eel grass or kelp. On their journey from spawning grounds to the saltwater shore, Chum fry may encounter and compete with other newly hatched fish: in particular, Pink Salmon (*Oncorhynchus gorbuscha*), the species to which Chum Salmon is most closely related, also exhibit a similar lifestyle, with the newly emerged young moving quickly downstream.

Feeding on zooplankton, Chum fry remain in shallow waters until July or August. At this time, the small fish began their perilous journey seaward, away from the shore. Most will not survive, but for those that do, within a few years they will turn landward towards their natal stream.

Fishing

Chum Salmon may not be considered a desirable main course by humans, but this does not mean that their soft, unappetizing flesh historically escaped notice by recreational and commercial fishers alike. In the earlyr years of the fishery, Chum Salmon were often in the "incidental take" category. The impact was more apparent than the name implies; for example, in 1974 a new commercial fishery in Hood Canal targeted towards Coho Salmon brought in unwanted species, such as the Chum. The bycatch number could be very high.

Directed Chum harvest in the canal began in 1976-1977, peaking in 1987 with a fishing rate of 90%, although by this time there were not many fish to be caught. Inevitably, the population had gone into a steep decline, and in 1993 the fishery was nearly nonexistent. Nevertheless, the harvest rate was 57% from 1974 through 1991. By 1992, the population was considered critical. Where previously found throughout this shallow sea, nearly half of the canal's streams no longer supported Chum Salmon.

Thus, when petitions for listing the summer-run Hood Canal Chum Salmon - an Evolutionary Significant Unit (ESU) that includes the Strait of Juan de Fuca west to the Dungeness River - were first introduced the number in the canal was approximately three percent of its former abundance.

Fisheries were also active in the Strait and the San Juan Islands, the latter averaging 1,600 adults from 1990-1991. The decline in Chum numbers in the Strait began approximately 10 years later than in Hood Canal, with the number lowest in 1989: it is estimated that the run size that year was 425 fish. Some rebound occurred in the early 1990s when hatchery-bred salmon augmented the population and harvesting was more restricted. Commercial fishing in Discovery Bay and Sequim Bay ended in 1976, but today harvesting, primarily of fall-run spawning fish, in the Strait has continued. Fishing is permitted for Threatened ESUs.

Today, millions of Chum Salmon are caught annually on the outer coast in both Washington and British Columbia; these fish are of mixed origin, having traveled from freshwater spawning locations throughout the Salish Sea.

Chum Salmon numbers, both hatchery and natural origin fish, tend to vary widely, often on a year- to-year basis. Both the summer-run Hood Canal threatened ESU and the fall-run Chum are subject to such fluctuations. It is this sensitivity to environmental conditions, of which understanding is limited, that continues to make the species challenging to managers.

In the port of Seattle, Chum Salmon is one of the top ten seafood exports. The flesh is most often canned or smoked. The fishery is considered a "good seafood choice with sustainable harvest." Unfortunately, the Hood Canal summer-run Chum can contribute little to such a reassuring assessment.

Circled Life

Decline

Intensive Chum fishing certainly played a role in the free fall of the Hood Canal summer run, but many other factors contributed as well. While natural occurrences, such as landslides or floods, can stress fish populations, these are usually events from which recovery takes place within a few years. Long term, the most deleterious factors tend to be attributable to human activities.

With the Olympic Mountain range on the west, hills on the east, and a long sinuous form, Hood Canal is a beautiful place and understandably desirable for development and resource exploitation. Much of the shoreline is populated, and thus has been altered in many ways. Impacts from pollution, and modifications to streams and rivers, such as dike building, are inevitable without control. For example, dikes built illegally alongside the Big Quilcene River altered 1,700 feet of Chum Salmon spawning habitat.

Other activities contributing to habitat destruction include logging, farming, application of herbicides and pesticides, and removal of woody debris. Poaching, marine mammal increase and predation, eutrophication, loss of protective fry cover such as eelgrass beds, and interactions with hatchery fish — all these and more contribute to the depression of Chum numbers. The impact of such activities may not have been predicted, but the reality of the destruction of spawning sites offers a lesson.

This list of societal-induced changes that have reduced the Hood Canal Chum summer-run is sadly very long and constitutes an indictment of human impacts on all salmon species and other fish as well. Such human activities also exacerbate environmental factors: these include but are not limited to fluctuations in ocean conditions, climate change, and localized natural events, such as floods and landslides.

The impact of such changes may not have been predicted, but

the results offer a lesson.

A much larger body of water than Hood Canal, the Strait of Juan de Fuca gives the impression of being less impacted by human activities. Yet rivers, streams, and saltwater alike have been significantly altered. Chum Salmon have been on the decline for years, and when a listing of the Hood Canal summer-run Chum as Endangered was sought, it would include the Chum populations of the eastern Strait.

Listing

On March 25, 1999, under the provisions of the Endangered Species Act (ESA) of 1973, the National Marine Fisheries Service (NMFS), a department of the Oceanic and Atmospheric Administration (NOAA) issued a final ruling on two Chum Salmon Evolutionary Significant Units (ESUs). These two ESUs were the Hood Canal summer-run and the Columbia River Chum. Both were ultimately designated as Threatened. In the ruling, Discovery, Sequim, and Dungeness Bays, all of them geographical features of the Strait, were included in the Hood Canal summer-run ESU. Only wild Chum living below natural, impassable barriers, were considered in the listing. This specification implied that hybrids between hatchery and salmon that are "naturally spawned" were not considered part of the ESU.

Previous conservation efforts, if present, would be considered in proposals for regulations and recovery plans. It is interesting to note, however, that exceptions to harvest rules implied by a listing could be made in areas with conservation plans; such populations might be considered healthy, and thus exempt from protection.

Although less restrictive in protective measures than an Endangered status, a threatened ESU is nevertheless considered likely to become endangered if factors contributing to its decline are not addressed. For the summer-run Chum the proclamation became effective on May 24, 1999. This listing set in motion required documentation and subsequent actions that would hopefully lead to recovery and delisting.

The determination was made five years after the initial petition, which was filed by the Professional Resources Organization-Salmon (PRO-Salmon). A second petition, dated April 4, 1994, was submitted by the Save Allison Springs Citizens Committee — in this case the petition was specific to Puget Sound streams. A third was filed by Trout Unlimited, requesting listing for summer-run chum in 12 Hood Canal tributaries. The NMFS was thus directed to consider those specific waterways, while not being restricted to them.

Within a few months following the submittals, the NMFS announced that sufficient scientific evidence had been provided to begin protection and status reviews; these would consider all Chum Salmon populations. During this time public comments were solicited, and scientific evaluation was undertaken by the Biological Review Team (BRT). In March of 1998, four years after petitioning, the listing of the two ESUs was proposed.

At least one public response to the proposal concerned the exclusion of the Dungeness River summer-run Chum from the listing. In response, the run was included when the listing was made, with the NMFS citing the availability of new data on the Dungeness as a factor in the decision.

As part of the proposal review, the NMFS investigated the protective efforts being undertaken for summer-run Chum Salmon, noting that the Hood Canal/Strait of Juan de Fuca Chum Salmon Conservation Plan (HCSCP) was at the time the most comprehensive conservation plan at an ESU scale. NMFS was directed to encourage the continuation of this program.

Also noted was hatchery supplementation and reintroduction efforts to the recovery of the two ESUs. This included programs undertaken to enhance dwindling Chum Salmon numbers in smaller Strait water courses such as Snow Creek, Salmon Creek, and Jimmycomelately Creek.

At the time of listing, the Hood Canal summer-run Chum Salmon count was less than 1,000 adult fish: in 1968, it was 43,720.

Restoration/Conservation Part I – Before Listing

Although conservation efforts were not considered adequate to protect an ESU, prior to the listing organizations committed to restoration and conservation of local Chum Salmon populations were active. In 1986, a small group of people committed to three basic principles — Education, Celebration, and Restoration — formed the Wild Olympic Salmon (WOS). From the start, WOS included people of diverse backgrounds and occupations, and activities such as festivals and artistic endeavors would play important roles in creating a sense of community and purpose. In 1988, WOS was instrumental in the creation of Fin, a 13-foot hollow, portable salmon sculpture on wheels, with a mural painted inside. Since its introduction to the public, FIN has traveled as far as the nation's capital while continuing to play an important local role in education for young and old alike. At festivals, parades, and other public celebrations FIN is truly an emissary for salmon awareness.

A large sculpture such as FIN plays an important role in public awareness, but in 1987 the reality of the concerns she would represent became very real at Chimacum Creek, a local salmon-bearing stream that empties into Port Townsend Bay. Chimacum Creek had supported a Chum Salmon run in the past; now spawning fish no longer returned to the creek.

Two primary causes of the extirpation of the Chum Salmon in Chimacum Creek were implicated — a significant flood in 1987 that destroyed a culvert at the mouth of the creek, and a logging road upstream. Sediment from the event and the road effectively eliminated the Chum Salmon run in the lower reaches of the creek. The salmon were gone. Any celebration for the yearly return would be put on hold; the question was what, if anything, could be done to reverse the catastrophe.

The loss of the Chum in Chimacum Creek would not only result in WOS involvement in an unprecedented restoration effort but also contribute to the formation of the Jefferson Land Trust (JLT). By 1989, the JLT would implement a commitment to conservation with land use alterations, whether through easements or purchase.

Both WOS and JLT as well as other organizations such as the Washington Department of Fish and Wildlife (WDFW) became involved with a restoration project on Chimacum Creek. Since the run was extinct, the closest available Chum stock that could be used for reintroduction was the population at Salmon Creek, a stream that emptied into Discovery Bay.

In response to WOS efforts to restore the Chimacum Creek run, a supplementation program was begun at Salmon Creek. A small Chum population, also considered at high risk, would serve as broodstock for reintroduction at both Chimacum and Salmon Creek. In 1992, a few adults were trapped near the mouth of Salmon Creek and held for spawning. Following egg collection, fertilization and incubation were undertaken at the Dungeness Hatchery. Otoliths (ear bones) were marked, and the eggs then transferred to incubators at a hatchery on Houck Creek. Here the hatched fry were fed for two weeks and at a specified weight released into Discovery Bay at the mouth of Salmon Creek. By 2001, the fry were being freed directly into freshwater.

In 1996 a similar program was begun at Chimacum Creek, with incubation of Salmon Creek Chum eggs at a hatchery on Naylors Creek, a tributary. Fry were released into Port Townsend Bay near the mouth of Chimacum Creek; in 1999 adults were observed, the first in 12 years.

Oncorhynchus keta - Chum

At Jimmycomelately Creek, a small stream that empties into Sequim Bay, a similar program was begun in 1999. This supplementation effort involved trapping of adults returning to the creek and subsequent fertilization and incubation at Hurd Creek Hatchery on the Dungeness River. Eggs were transferred to a tributary of Jimmycomelately where they were hatched. Fry were released into the creek near its mouth.

In 2002, approximately 850 natural origin spawners returned to Chimacum Creek: meanwhile, at Salmon Creek nearly 1,500 spawning Chum were counted.

By 2003, the effective population size — that is, the size that participates in production of the next generation, a number much less than the total run — had increased to more than twelve times its pre-supplementation number. The program was considered so successful that supplementation was discontinued.

Thus, when the summer-run Hood Canal salmon was listed in March 1999, programs were in place on two creeks and beginning at a third.

The success of these carefully managed and documented hatching programs could be measured in numbers and continuing returns. Chum Salmon were back in creeks that had been their home for thousands of years. It was cause for celebration, particularly for the commitment of individuals and groups whose unselfish efforts had met with success.

The North Olympic Salmon Coalition (NOSC)

Other conservation and restoration programs had also begun prior to the 1999 Chum Salmon summer-run listing; these efforts are ongoing today. In 1990, the Washington State legislature passed a law creating the Regional Fisheries Enhancement Group Program (RFEG). This program was responsible for the formation of 14 RFEGs throughout the state. The goal was salmon recovery, a process that was mandated to include diverse groups of people, such as volunteers, landowners, tribal members, and communities. Funding for these groups would come from fishing license fees as well as grants and local programs. Under this directive, the North Olympic Salmon Coalition (NOSC) was formed. This organization would merge with WOS and undertake protection and restoration programs involving all Olympic Peninsula salmon-bearing water bodies.

Since its creation in 1990, NOSC has become a leader of salmon restoration actions throughout the region. With a small paid staff and a large contingent of volunteers and concerned citizens, prior to the Hood Canal listing NOSC had been involved with projects such as the Salmon Creek salmon supplementation program (in conjunction with WOS). NOSC had also implemented revegetation projects, such as those at Chimacum Creek, and was instrumental in the Snow Creek restoration effort. Beginning in April 1996, this extensive project involved lowering the streambed, planting native species to restore riparian vegetation, and installing structures for stabilization. It would benefit the summer-run Chum as well as Steelhead and Coho.

By 1997, NOSC was expanding its activities, with plans to implement eight new enhancement projects the following year. The organization was gaining experience, monetary support, and, importantly, a community of volunteers and locally engaged supporters. Through its early efforts, NOSC was poised to become increasingly involved with salmon restoration after the listing of the summer-run Chum in 1999.

Restoration/Conservation Part II – After Listing

While some efforts are directed at the newly listed Chum, restoration projects on the Olympic Peninsula in the 21st century often benefit all salmon species: likewise, programs in place for other species can promote the health of Chum Salmon runs. Proposals by NOSC, in conjunction with other organizations such as WDFW and JLT, have been numerous, and involve several approaches to restoration, such as land acquisition and conservation easements, native plantings to restore streamside vegetation, fish monitoring of juveniles and spawning adults, culvert replacements, and reconfiguration of stream channels. Educational programs to promote public awareness and inclusion of local students are also part of the approach to building healthy salmon runs; these and other endeavors are an acknowledgement of the importance of community involvement.

Time and effort, and money as well, have added to the enhancement of many projects in place prior to 1999, while new proposals, begun with commitment to both short and long-term goals, have been submitted. For example, between 1999 and 2001, aided by grants, NOSC worked on more than 20 projects.

Some of the projects since listing have been small in scale and of short duration; others are long term. One such effort involved the acquisition of property bordering the Dungeness River a few miles from the mouth. The Jamestown S'Klallam Tribe took a leadership role by using available funds to both purchase land and begin restoration of sites along the river. Alterations to the Dungeness from activities such as channeling, road construction, levees, and more had degraded the river and its floodplain, making it marginal as salmon habitat. Acquisition of four properties totaling 21.44 acres of riverine habitat was completed in 2017. This purchase included 1.03 miles of river frontage, beginning at Highway 101 (6.5 miles from the river's mouth) and extending to river mile 10.5. The goal of land management for these parcels was restoration of salmon habitat in a stretch of the river that is within the migration zone for spawning salmon, including the summer-run threatened Chum Salmon as well as listed Chinook, Bull Trout, and Steelhead. Also present in the river were non-listed Coho Salmon, Pink Salmon, and Fall Chum.

Thus, as with many properties acquired for restoration, enhancement projects would benefit all salmon species.

Of the four newly acquired restoration properties, one — the Caldero property, purchased in 2017 — was considered a high priority site and subsequently proposed for restoration. Located between mileposts 9.5 and 10.5, Caldero was a much-altered 7.85-acre property. The Dungeness flows rapidly in the area, and thus restoration proposals included alterations to the river's course. A side channel would be dug to provide slower flows; additionally, strategically placed engineered log jams would increase habitat for salmon adults and juveniles as well; the reduced main flow would also be slowed with the addition of four additional log jams.

The physical work involved in restoring a site was not limited to moving rocks, digging channels, and structure emplacement. Caldero is a broad, flat piece of land and, although not logged commercially, the vegetation cover lacked diversity. The soil reflected a history of river incursions with much clay and hardpan, and rocks small and large dotted the landscape.

Yet despite the hard substrate, this was a place where restoration could go beyond riverbanks to encompass much of the site. It was an arena in which volunteers could contribute time and effort by planting native species.

in 2022, citizens numbering in the hundreds began digging and planting thousands of trees and shrubs. In the spring of 2023 alone, a goal of 12,000 plants was implemented, and in the early winter of 2023 alone more than 6,700 were dug into their new home.

The hope for survival of plants through all the seasons is strong amongst those involved with streamside restoration, and the unprecedented alterations to the swift Dungeness River represent a step forward in the attempt to return an unproductive landscape to one which benefits both salmon and other species — including humans — alike. As a large-scale project, Caldero represents a step forward in the quest to save wild salmon.

Fall-run Chum Salmon — the Elwha

The fall-run Chum Salmon in the Elwha was for the most part considered to be of natural origin although there had been a hatchery program from 1975 to 1985. Prior to dam removal, the Chum population varied widely, with as many as 1,000 fish in 2008. Although supplementation began again following construction of the Lower Elwha Klallam Tribe (LEKT) House of Salmon, located near the mouth of the river, today fisheries personnel do not consider this species to be recovered in the river, although spawning adults have been seen in the upper portion near the Glines Canyon dam site. In 2022, the population estimate was 390. Such a low number seems at odds with an expected increase following dam removal. And since Chum Salmon typically spawn in lower river reaches, the species should benefit directly from improved habitat.

However, the Chum fall-run was nearly decimated during the dam removal process. In 2013, sediment released as the Glines Canyon dam was taken down had a severe impact on all species, including the Chum. That year the annual smolt count, an effort that was begun in 2006, was halted because of the sediment damage to the traps and subsequent fish mortality.

An important tool for assessing recovery in the Elwha, the smolt survey has continued to the present, providing an important tool for quantifying the recolonization of the river and its tributaries following dam removal. For the Chum, the slow return is thus documented.

At the present time, the hope for Chum Salmon expansion in numbers and range rests in hatchery production, specifically at the House of Salmon. Returns to the hatchery reflect the low numbers of spawning fish in the Elwha. With fewer than ten adults, the number of eggs that can be incubated is correspondingly much less than for other salmon species: in 2024, approximately 5,000 fry will be released in early spring. Of these, a small percentage will return as adults in 3 to 4 years.

The goal of Elwha River hatcheries is to both increase and stabilize species such as the Chum Salmon to the point that supplementation will no longer be required to maintain a viable population. Such has been the outcome in summer-run chum populations in streams east of the much-altered Elwha River. From the efforts of many, including those with the vision to restore habitat by the implementation of what could be considered an exceptionally radical plan in the late 20th century, the removal of the Elwha dams is a test case for restoration and conservation. It offers hope for the future.

Although 1,376 returning fish were counted, 2023 was not the best year for the Jimmycomelately Chum Salmon count. Tended seven days a week, in late October the trap was removed for another year. Chum were seen a mile upriver, a good sign of spawning habitat expansion. And compared to the past, when numbers brushed the near-zero mark, the return of the Chum was always welcomed.

Chum Salmon numbers do fluctuate widely from year to year, and so tempering optimism with caution seems prudent when evaluating restoration of the threatened summer-run. Restrictions, restoration, engagement, including counting — all are necessary human activities that support the preservation of what was nearly lost.

With the shortening of summer days, I look forward to being granted entry once again to that exotic, beautiful world of the returning salmon. The visit will be temporary, as it should be.

Oncorhynchus clarkii - Cutthroat

We stood on the Icicle River's banks, my dad and me. In his hand he held a long, bamboo rod, while in mine I gripped a small, stiff, fiberglass miniature.

"Are you ready"? he said.

"Sure."

We turned upriver, me clambering over boulders and rocks, while he, at over six feet tall, moved as though on a streamside path. No matter. I was young and nimble and he a man with depths of patience and concern for his youngest child. Together we were embarking on a demanding adventure, but one with deep rewards.

It wasn't long before we reached the first of many stops we would make that day. The bank flattened, as though to allow us easy access to the edge of an emerald-green pool, a perfect place for fish and the anglers who sought them.

The limit was 15 in those days, and the fish were small. For even at that time, what had once been a historic run of large fish was augmented by hatchery rainbows, the commonly released species in lakes and rivers across the West. Those were barely six inches in length, and when we caught one, we measured them carefully. Five-and-a-half inches would not do.

The pool yielded a couple of these small, beautiful creatures, intended for our dinner, but soon my dad grew impatient, and we moved on, continuing to navigate the banks of this white-and-green swift stream.

Another pause, this time at a larger pool. Dad settled on a large log at its edge and I on a smaller one nearer the water. I placed a salmon egg on the hook and cast the line outwards, over the center of the pool. And waited.

The tug on the pole was intense as the fishing line swept through the waters, its path a zigzag of unrepeatable pattern. This was clearly not a six-inch rainbow, but whatever it was the drive to be free was evident. I held on tight.

Dad clambered down and stood beside me, not aiding, but

suggesting.

And so, I reeled the fish to the surface of the water, close to us.

And then we saw the flash of red.
"A Cutthroat," my dad exclaimed. "Not a common fish at all!"
He smiled.
We held it briefly in our hands. I saw the red "slashes" on its belly. A way to signal another fish in the dark waters?
The hook was almost loose, the fish almost free. I carefully extracted the remaining tip.
It left so quickly, and disappeared so completely into the pool's depths, that the experience seemed a dream. But not quite. I can close my eyes and see the fish, accented with red, vitally alive with a determination we earthbound creatures can only envy.

With a common name derived from the two red streaks beneath its jaws, as a member of the *Oncorhynchus* genus and the Salmonidae family, technically the Cutthroat Trout is a salmon. And whereas its cousins, such as the mighty Chinook (*Oncorhynchus tshawytscha*) or the muscle-bound Chum (*O. keta*) embrace an anadromous lifestyle that promises death after spawning, as a youngster the Cutthroat might adopt one of four distinct lifestyles, none of them necessarily implying demise at their place of birth.

However, for the Cutthroat, this life choice is not necessarily binding. Giving the impression of being stuck in an identity crises, the individual fish might embrace the annual saltwater sojourn, only departing to spawn in shallow freshwater streams. Or sometimes it skips the journey to its natal home, or migrates partway, halting in a rich estuary. If denied access to the sea altogether, it may spend a lifetime in pools and riffles above inaccessible waterfalls, safe from incursions. Or there is always a lake for a committed home stay, or perhaps an exclusively

Oncorhynchus clarkii - Cutthroat

freshwater stream existence.

As an acknowledgement of its wide distribution and varying habitat preferences, the Cutthroat is divided into several subspecies - 14 according to one source. Most subspecies, including two in Washington state, do not have access to saltwater. Cutthroat in the Strait, however, belong to the coastal population. Named subspecies *clarkii*, these are fish of cold streams and rivers that drain to saltwater, where they spend part of their lives.

Oncorhynchus clarkii - Cutthroat Trout

For a salmon, the Cutthroat is small, although at least one was measured at more than 30 inches (76 cm) and tilted the scales at 17 pounds. A more average length is 8-10 inches with a maximum weight of 1.4 pounds, although Coastal Cutthroat are sometimes over a foot in length. The body is elongated and fusiform, the head and eyes large, with an upper jaw that extends beyond the eye. The inside of the mouth is white, the teeth numerous, with a few at the base of the tongue. Sea-run fish are greenish blue to blue-black on the back, with silvery sides and belly. During spawning season, males develop slightly hooked jaws. The fish are darkened on the back, fins, head, and sides with small black spots.

Most prominent, and a mark that distinguishes the Cutthroat from all others, are the two red slashes on the underside of the lower jaw.

Absent in waters west of the Bering Sea, Cutthroat is strictly a North American species. The several subspecies range across the continental interior, while the Coastal Cutthroat is at home from the Kenai peninsula in Alaska southward along the coast to British Columbia, Washington, Oregon, and northern California. The Cutthroat resides throughout the Columbia River drainage, east to Colorado, and south to Arizona. There are three subspecies in Washington; these include the Coastal (subspecies *clarkii*), the Westslope (subspecies *lewisii*), and the Lahontan (subspecies *henshawi*). The Coastal *clarkii* is distributed most widely and is also the only anadromous subspecies.

Like other *Oncorhynchus*, Cutthroat prefer cold water, spawning in temperatures as low as 43° F (6.1° C), and although they will tolerate higher, this fish does not thrive in waters greater than 48° F (8.9° C). They mature in 3-4 years but can live as long as 10 years. Females lay from 100 to at least 4,420 eggs, which hatch in 28-40 days: the young stay beneath the gravel for 1-2 weeks. Cutthroat juveniles remain in freshwater for 1-9 years, with an average of 3 years. Not all migrate to salt water, but for those coastal fish that do, some will travel offshore as far as 31 miles (50 km). But for the most part this is a salmon that stays close to its natal river, coming and going from saltwater to fresh, motivated by unseen and poorly understood forces, although certainly prey availability must play a role.

These back-and-forth tendencies, including spawning runs to their birthplace and forays in the sea, imply that spawning does not necessarily result in death: the Cutthroat is thus an iteroparous species, one that can reproduce more than once in its lifetime. One study reported that up to 40% survive to repeat spawning, with a record of five for a 10-year-old individual.

An Honorary Name

While the "cutthroat" designation refers to the red streaks on the lower jaw, the species' scientific name — *clarkii* — honors William Clark, the co-leader of the Lewis and Clark expedition of 1804-1806. Camped near Fort Mandan on the Missouri River the first winter, in the spring of 1805, the Corps continued their journey northwest, reaching Great Falls in July. Hunting for mammals to replenish their supplies and satisfy their appetites, Clark originally indicated an absence of fish above the falls but did note the presence of more than one trout species at the base. When one of the expedition members returned with a bountiful catch (the Corps would sometimes feast on a few hundred fish), Clark described two of the species in some detail. For one, he mentions the distinctive teeth on the tongue, the wide mouth, and the bluish color. It is not completely clear whether he was describing the fish that would become his namesake, although it has been interpreted by historians as such. Lewis, however, clearly identified the Cutthroat, mentioning the teeth and the "small dash of red."

By the third decade of the 19th century, the Cutthroat was given scientific recognition and named *Salmo clarkii* by Sir John Richardson after he received specimens from Fort Vancouver on the Columbia River. A Scottish physician who had traveled extensively in Canada in the company of the John Franklin, the famous explorer later lost in the search for the Northwest Passage, Richardson believed these specimens to be the same species referred to by Clark as "a dark variety of salmon-trout." Thus, Clark was honored with the name, while Richardson would author a well-known book about North American fauna.

Circled Life

Eventually Richardson would give up the explorer's life and retire to Scotland.

While the designation as a *Salmo* implied a close relationship to the well-known Atlantic Salmon *(Salmo salar)*, in 1989 the affinity with western North American salmon species was acknowledged, and the Cutthroat was renamed as a salmon — *Oncorhynchus,* meaning "hooked jaw," in reference to the male's protruding lower jaw.

Evolution

Most closely related to Steelhead *(Oncorhynchus mykiss)* and the Asian Cherry Salmon *(O. masou)*, the Cutthroat separated from other genus members approximately 5.3 million years ago near the end of the Miocene Epoch, and a couple of million years before the Pleistocene, a cold epoch often referred to as the Ice Age. Thus, although primarily a cold-water species, the Cutthroat species recognized today evolved prior to the onset of the ice sheets that would reshape much of the Northern Hemisphere.

This Pleistocene was a time of great challenges and opportunities for Earth's flora and fauna. With the evolution of several modern animal groups, many would flourish during glacial maximums. As for the fish, pushed southward as the ice locked up more land, their pliability and resilience promised a future of opportunistic responses as the ice retreated. While the largest of earthbound creatures went extinct, salmon such as the Cutthroat and its "hooked jaw" relatives were poised for adaptation and radiation into a landscape of new rivers, streams, saltwater inlets, and cold lakes. With its flexible approach to living and dying, the Cutthroat's future was bright indeed.

Complex Lifestyles

Four lifestyles — iteroparous, adfluvial, fluvial, and resident

Oncorhynchus clarkii - Cutthroat

— are most often recognized for the Cutthroat. "Iteroparous" refers to the life course of those fish born in streams that drain to salt water, such as the Coastal Cutthroat; these individuals may travel between the two habitats several times during their lives. "Adfluvial" means individuals that spawn in tributary streams, with the juveniles migrating to a lake and maturing in that habitat. "Fluvial" Cutthroat are those that spawn in a stream and mature in a river. "Resident" fish are those isolated in river reaches or lake environments. What is most interesting about this species is that for individuals with access to more than one habitat, such as the coastal environment, preference is not always consistent, particularly for the form that makes its home in the Strait.

The smallest of the widespread Cutthroat, the Coastal subspecies has access to saltwater, where it most often remains close to its natal river. However, it is not a simple migration pattern, with birth in a stream, movement through an estuary to a saltwater habitat, and a return upriver a couple of years later to spawn. Some individuals may start their journey upstream, only to stay for a time in the estuary, perhaps to take advantage of available food, and then return to saltwater, forgoing spawning altogether. Or a fish might migrate to its natal home but decline to spawn. Stream juvenile residency is also variable, and older fish tend to reach spawning areas before younger.

Fall and winter runs have both been identified for the Coastal Cutthroat. In early autumn, adults tend to migrate to large streams, while December and January spawners prefer small tributaries that drain directly to saltwater. Spawning usually takes place from December to February. Most return migrations to estuaries and saltwater occur from April through June. Cutthroat most often overwinter in freshwater.

The density of Cutthroat redds (nests) tends to be lower than for other salmon. Juveniles emerging from their gravelly birthplace feed on invertebrates, while in estuarine and saltwater environments maturing fish prey on other fishes, including young Coho and Chum salmon, and smaller fishes such as herrings, sculpins, and sand lance. Other predators find Cutthroat delectable; Pacific hake, spiny dogfish, and larger salmon eat them, as well as seals.

Cutthroat in the Strait

As the only iteroparous Cutthroat, subspecies *clarkii* is found throughout western Washington and Oregon. It ranges from the Cascades to the coast, including the lower Columbia River and those rivers and streams that drain to the Salish Sea. On the Peninsula, *clarkii* lives in large riverswith headwaters located in the Olympic Mountains; these include Pacific coast rivers, such as the Quinault and Hoh, as well as major rivers along the Strait — the Hoko, Elwha, Dungeness, Sekiu, and Lyre. Most often spawning in shallow streams, the coastal form forays into familiar creeks, such as Snow, Salmon, Jimmycomelately, Johnson, and unnamed tributaries as well. The numbers of returning fish are small, and for many waterways Cutthroat distribution is poorly understood.

This deficiency in Cutthroat data is due in part to the absence of a commercial fishery; thus, funding that supports research into more lucrative salmon species is not as readily available for this small fish. Information concerning life history, population dynamics, and genetics, such as the impact of hybridization with other salmonids, is limited. Some work has been done, however, including a salmonid stock inventory (SaSI), undertaken in the early 21st century by the Washington Department of Fish and Wildlife (WDFW). This survey identified forty stock "complexes" defined as closely related populations in a single watershed. In the eastern Strait of Juan de Fuca, several small creeks, tributaries to both Discovery and Sequim Bays, were included in the regional stock complex. These are natural origin fish, genetically distinct

Oncorhynchus clarkii - Cutthroat

from Midstrait and Western Strait stock complexes.

In fact, the division of the coastal Cutthroat Trout into six Evolutionarily Significant Units (ESU) reveals this distinction between eastern and western Strait populations. The eastern fish are part of the Puget Sound ESU, which extends north into the Strait of Georgia. The western distribution includes the rest of the Olympic Peninsula, with a southern boundary near the Chehalis River on the coast. The concept of the ESU is important for conservation, particularly for Endangered Species Act (ESA) listing. However, it does not specify the genetic distinctions between local Cutthroat populations.

Fishing the Cutthroat

As mentioned above, historically the Cutthroat has not been commercially fished. It is known to have been locally consumed by tribes along the coast and today can be caught in subsistence fisheries. For regulation purposes, the Cutthroat is a "trout" and in saltwater is a "catch-and-release" fish only. Mortality from such fishing activity is believed to be low, although it is not quantified.

In rivers and streams Cutthroat is a popular fish for anglers, considered both tasty and worth pursuing for its vigorous objection to being hooked. The minimum allowed size is 8 inches, and the daily limit is two fish, including all species of trout. In lakes, ponds, and reservoirs any size may be kept, with a limit of 5 each day during the season.

There are "special rules" that limit size, in an effort to promote spawning for at least one cycle. For example, the Dungeness River is open from Oct. 16-Jan. 31, with retention permitted for those fish 14 inches or more. The Elwha River is closed to fishing, while fish caught in the Hoko are also restricted in size, and during autumn only fly fishing is allowed. Anglers are required to follow all rules, including "special" designations, and are regulated for the type of tackle they can use.

Circled Life

Lakes are often supplemented with hatchery fish, typically numbering in the thousands. Those lakes on the north Olympic Peninsula where Cutthroat are present include Beaver, Dickey, Pleasant, Sutherland, and Wentworth. Except for Lake Sutherland, which is restricted to spring and summer, these small water bodies are open to Cutthroat fishing throughout the year.

Overfishing was one of the culprits in the decline of Coastal Cutthroat during the 1980s and 1990s; such a dismaying reality represented a culmination of the increased popularity of the fish, beginning in the 1960s. In 1974, a survey in Puget Sound revealed the cutthroat was second only to salmon as a preferred catch. Anglers numbered in the tens of thousands in marine waters, their expenditures making significant contributions to the local economy.

Fishing pressure is one of several factors often noted for the impact on many fish species, including the Cutthroat. Habitat destruction, increasing logging with its practices that often result in stream and river degradation, population growth, and other impacts must continually be addressed in the efforts to maintain healthy populations of the seven *Oncorhynchus* species native to Pacific Northwest marine and freshwater habitats. This reality is reflected in the tightening of fishing regulations: in 1983, the Cutthroat limit dropped from 12 to 8, and by 1986 the maximum take per day in marine waters was two trout. The loss had been noted in creel census data; at that time direct surveys were lacking.

Hatchery Augmentation

Retaining Coastal Cutthroat in marine waters is not permitted, but along with the Westslope and Lahontan subspecies, hatchery production offers an annual opportunity for anglers to catch this favorite fish. Except for the Cowlitz River, releases are confined to lakes. A handful of state facilities raise Cutthroat to the smolt stage, releasing them in spring and summer for the recreational fishery. The number varies from the hundreds to the tens of thousands between sites; however, annual supplementation is greatest east of the Cascades.

Examples of release numbers proposed for the 2024-2025 seasons include 195,000 Westslope Cutthroat to Kittitas County lakes, 5,000 to Okanogan County Lakes, and 2,000 to Skamania County Lakes, all eastern Washington counties. Approximately 200,000 will be released into Lake Chelan, a long, cold lake nestled in the mountainous desert. For lakes near the coast, the Eells Springs Hatchery, located south of Hood Canal in the Skokomish River drainage, which terminates in the Canal, provides much of the Cutthroat stock, with proposals of planting 19,000 in San Juan County lakes and 35,000 to Whatcom County, among others.

At the present time, hatchery Cutthroat are not released into Clallam County lakes, but fishing is possible in the few where resident populations are established. Near the Strait in Jefferson County, Lake Leland is augmented annually with both Cutthroat and Rainbow trout.

Since Cutthroat releases are primarily for lakes, concern over mixing with sea-run Cutthroat is minimal. Continued annual fishing opportunities are, at the present time, dependent on hatchery production. This effort takes pressure off natural origin fish, hopefully contributing to their slow increase.

Meandering Fish

The variable lifestyles embraced by the Coastal Cutthroat offer a challenge to scientists and anglers alike. Understanding the many factors influencing the population is paramount for ensuring the future of this enigmatic fish. Research into hybridization of Cutthroat with both the anadromous saltwater and freshwater (Rainbow) Steelhead forms has provided some insight into hybrid movements and fertility in coastal freshwater and saltwater environments. Investigation of prey preferences has been informative for its possible impact on other salmon species, for although small, the Cutthroat is very cosmopolitan in its diet.

One of the most interesting observations of Coastal Cutthroat behavior has been on Indian Creek, a tributary to the Elwha River. Perhaps attributable to the dam removals on the Elwha that transformed its waters to a free-flowing state for the first time in nearly a century, in 2014 Cutthroat were observed spawning in the creek in October and November, early for a trout that typically spawns in spring. The Cutthroat were present by the hundreds, or more, and surveys located many redds. Cool autumn water temperatures may have contributed to good spawning conditions, although the flows in the upper stream are variable, like the Elwha itself. Farther downstream, "normal" springtime spawning Cutthroat were found.

The autumn-spawning Cutthroat were not the only species to utilize Indian Creek. Coho salmon present in the stream preyed on small cutthroat and may have disturbed cutthroat redds in the creek. However, according to one researcher, the spawning Cutthroat population has persisted.

The reason for this unusual spawning event may be unknown, but south and east of the Elwha, some studies have revealed Cutthroat site fidelity. One survey revealed that a southern Puget Sound group of 120 Cutthroat remained in the Sound, and most were resident in shoreline habitats, feeding mainly at night in shallow water.

Such a tendency to sedentary behavior has been traced in other Cutthroat populations. On the coast, remaining near the natal stream is the norm, with entry into salt water most common at age two to three. Cutthroat do not stay at sea; the sojourn there probably offers an increased opportunity for varied prey.

Yet if an individual fish chooses, it might alter its lifestyle, remaining in a stream or lake, perhaps spawning or not, with travelers mingling with other populations, and an occasion,

Oncorhynchus clarkii - **Cutthroat**

hybridizing with relatives. Considered a "keystone species" by some researchers, although flexible in lifestyle, the Cutthroat retains its demands for cool water, protection, and sufficient prey. Nearly extirpated in some regions of the West, whether its adaptability can ameliorate impacts of warming waters remains to be seen. In the meantime, whether in a lake, a river, or a nearshore saltwater environment, a wild Cutthroat encounter is memorable. A survivor of ice in the past and rapid warming in the present, a Cutthroat offers hope for itself and other water-bound creatures as well. With a genetic signature older than humanity, it goes about the business of eating and breathing, spawning and competing, interacting only when unavoidable with the younger, two-legged being that, whether intending to or not, holds the fish's future in its hands.

Alongside a stream that held an importance far greater than its small size suggested, I waited for the fish. These were smolts, most of them Coho, and all bound for the sea. In the company of other volunteers and fisheries' personnel, my assignment was to count those fish, and to do so with as little disturbance as possible. Each young animal was important, both for its presence and its future contribution to its species' survival.

Occasionally a large "kelt" would enter the holding area, possibly a repeat spawner or one returning to the sea. And, uncommonly as well, a solitary youngster, spotted rather than plain, big mouthed and vigorous, and, most importantly, brightened with red "slashes" along the jaw, would enter a net sized for smaller smolt but sufficiently large to hold the 10-inch fish.

Here it was — a Cutthroat. Exclaiming about its beauty, we identified and counted that fish, noting its contribution to a small run. Then we let it go, back into the stream of its birth. With its unintended role in the human goal of understanding and preserving, it did not delay its departure. The Cutthroat returned

Circled Life

to the stream, the brief interlude forgotten. Food and avoidance were on its mind, both best attained in salty waters, only a short swim in the cold waters of an inviting stream.

Oncorhynchus tshawytscha - Chinook

In the past, a great salmon entered the cold waters of the Strait, swimming ever upstream, answering an ancient call with a fleeting presence to those who observed its passing. Yet it was they who acknowledged its importance to their lives with a name reserved for the largest of its kind — the "Tyee." In the company of smaller companions, each year the Tyee provided sustenance for those who waited. The return provided sufficient food for a long winter, for this was a temporary passing. With a mixture of relief and thanksgiving, the people took many, while most passed by, forgoing food in a race against time, bound for the rivers where they had begun their lives only a few years before. There, in the swift freshwater of their birth, the great Tyee would spawn and die, passing on its uniqueness to tiny offspring it would never see.

Today, we know this salmon as the "Chinook," or the "King." For the most part, those great Tyee are consigned to memory, with the occasional photo a reminder of what once was. Most Chinook now begin their lives in an environment far removed and more controlled, rather than the swift waters that once defined their lives.

The largest of all Salmonidae family species, the Chinook Salmon — also called the King, the Blackmouth, the Spring, and the "Tyee," for the heaviest and longest of all — is today amongst the most imperiled of all north Pacific salmon. Delicious and nutritious, in the past it was a much sought-after fish for tribal fisheries and, with the arrival of settlers in the nineteenth century, in the historical record as well. Millions have been taken, so many that the largest fish are nearly consigned to memory, while today, rather than swimming up swift rivers that molded its evolution, the Chinook Salmon is more likely to return to a hatchery's placid waters.

Evolved in an environment conducive to size and strength, with a time frame extending back millions of years — much longer than humanity's existence — this is a fish that can tip the scales at 97 pounds, and measure 58 inches (147 cm) in length. Today, individuals weighing more than 50 pounds are rare. The average size is about 36 inches (90 cm) in length and 22 pounds.

Fusiform in shape, the adult Chinook has a large conical head, and a forward-directed wide mouth. Sea-run fish are metallic blue to green above, with silvery sides and white below. The dorsal fin and both lobes of the caudal fin are marked with small dark spots, and the body is spotted above the lateral line. The inside of the mouth is black.

As a mature Chinook enters the Strait and begins its journey towards freshwater, the body color darkens to an olive brown accented with a reddish or purplish hue. The male develops a hooked jaw (the genus name, *Oncorhynchus*, refers to this form, while *Tsahwytscha* is a Kamchatkan name), lined with large teeth. Called a "kype," this structure distinguishes the male and is indicative of the aggressive behavior it exhibits in its spawning

***Oncorhynchus tshawytscha* - Chinook**

Oncorhynchus tshawytscha - Chinook

habitat.

Ranging from northern Japan to the Russian far east and Kamchatka, across the Pacific to the Bering Sea, and south along the western coast of North America to central California, the Chinook is both widely distributed and adaptable. Prior to dam construction on the Columbia River, spawners returned upriver at least 560 miles (900 km), while in the Salish Sea, the great fish was at home in the shorter rivers that descend from the mountains to the sea. Far to the north, to return to its natal stream, the Chinook is known to travel up the Yukon River more than 1,860 miles (3,000 km).

Introduced from the freshwaters of the Great Lakes to the seas and hatcheries of New Zealand, and South America as well, the Chinook is native to the cold waters of the north Pacific. Emerging as a small fry from the gravels of freshwater rivers and streams, it is an anadromous fish that matures in saltwater, only to return to spawn in the stream where it was born where, its life mission complete, the spent fish dies within days.

Chinook are divided into two spawning runs — spring and fall. Spring Chinook ascend their natal rivers and streams in late May and early June, spawning in autumn: Fall Chinook migrate in August and September and spawn through November, sometimes later. The returning adults tend to move upstream during the day.

Large females can produce over 17,000 eggs, although the number is most often less. Eggs are deposited in a redd (nest) dug by her in clean gravel beds. After fertilization, hatching occurs in 30-160 days, typically sooner in warm water. Chinook can tolerate waters below freezing but are most often at home in temperatures from 46-54° F (8-12° C).

After a residency in their natal river of a few months to more than a year, Chinook smolt begin their seaward journey, swimming downstream while undergoing the physiological changes that enable saltwater survival. With the adaptation complete, they move seaward, where they will remain for 3 to 4 years, although sometimes less, while occasionally residency lasts as long as 9 years. At sea, the maturing fish tend to forage in deep waters during fall and winter and move closer to the surface as the days lengthen. Chinook prey primarily on fish and invertebrates: in return, they are eaten by marine mammals, birds, and humans.

The Chinook is considered by many to be the tastiest of all Salish Sea salmon. Rich in fat, it is buttery and firm, and is prepared with methods that range from grilling to baking to frying in an open pan. The taste varies depending on the source, and the flesh can be reddish or white: reportedly the flavor is similar, although the red-fleshed fish commands a higher price. Big and delicious, it is understandable why this fish has been eagerly sought for thousands of years.

In the Strait of Juan de Fuca, the annual return of the Chinook from the Pacific was a welcomed event in large rivers, such as the Elwha and the Dungeness, and in smaller rivers as well. Often acknowledged with ceremony, people along the coast recognized the importance of the Chinook to their survival. And in the deeper past, it seems possible that the fish and the people returned simultaneously to the borders and waters of a deep channel carved by a recently melted ice lobe. Stabilized by 5,000 years of relatively constant conditions and capable of inhabiting a new home far from the refugia that had sustained them, the Chinook had a long history of adaptability to the waters of the Pacific Northwest. The people as well had thrived in the cold yet richly endowed land.

Evolution

As the only family of its order, the Salmonidae includes approximately 200 species of Northern Hemisphere, cold water fish. Migratory, they spend much of their lives in large water bodies, often salty, such as the Salish Sea. The *Oncorhynchus* genus is perhaps best known for both its historical significance and its distinctive lifestyle: these are a fish that live in fresh and salt waters, reaching maturity in the sea and returning upriver to spawn. Although the origins of such behavior are a subject of debate, the *Oncorhynchus* most likely separated from the *Salmo* — a large genus represented in North America by the Atlantic Salmon (*Salmo salar*) — into a distinct genus about 5-6 million years ago. Today, *Oncorhynchus* numbers 16 species; seven are native to the waters of the Pacific Northwest.

Following the separation of the two genera, at least one fish that makes the Chinook look like an average-sized trout, plied the waters of North America. Now extinct, this was the Spike-toothed Salmon (*Oncorhynchus rastrosus*), a giant fish more than six feet in length and weighing nearly 400 pounds. Roaming the waters of the West, fossils of the Spike-toothed have been unearthed from freshwater sites, where it apparently spawned, with males developing the large teeth common to extant species.

Three million years prior to the onset of the current Ice Age (the Pleistocene), the salmon species familiar to us today were firmly established in rivers that emptied into the north Pacific. And given their preference for cold waters, the onset of the Pleistocene may have been advantageous for salmon, possibly increasing their range, or at the very least ensuring excellent habitat. The downside of this scenario was that as time passed the encroaching ice sheet, a giant maw sometimes thousands of feet thick, engulfed waters and land alike across much of the continent. With water turned to ice, saltwater shores dropped to lower elevations, obliterating river courses. Plants and animals were pushed ever southward. And although some fish populations would survive in northern refugia, for the most part the salmon would occupy waters free of ice.

One such location was the ancient Columbia River. Altered in its northerly course by the encroaching ice, the river flowed across lava beds, cutting downward, creating waterfalls and cold lakes. Subjected to immense floods from the blocked waters of ancient Lake Missoula, the river consistently ran south and west, emptying as it does today into the Pacific Ocean. Deep channels in the ocean floor reveal the river's path across dry land at a time when ocean waves pounded a shoreline 400 feet lower than it is today.

Although impacted by ice age dynamics, the constancy of water flow from the mountains to the sea in the ancient Columbia River offered refuge to salmon species forced southward. Then, as the glaciers began their retreat from southern Puget Sound approximately 17,000 years ago, the warming waters provided new opportunities for the adaptable Chinook. While Columbia River populations continued to number in the millions, meandering fish moved north along the Pacific coast, straying into ice-free salt and freshwater bodies. Theirs was a return to an ancient home and an expansion into the new. In time, they would eventually reach the Strait, a landform carved by ice now retreating from the entire Salish Sea basin.

Chinook Salmon possibly retreated north as well as south as the ice advanced across North America. A refugia in the rivers of Beringia, the dryland extension of present-day Alaska, could have provided a haven for salmon. Such a sanctuary undoubtedly closed at times as coastal rivers were subjected to cycles of melting and icing over, but if present, salmon could have taken advantage of receding ice, particularly during interglacial periods.

Fishing — Ice Age Salmon

Indigenous fishing of Chinook Salmon can be dated to the waning centuries of the Ice Age. In Alaska, fish bones of the related Chum Salmon (*Oncorhynchus keta*) are dated at 11,500 years old, making them amongst the earliest evidence of

Oncorhynchus tshawytscha - Chinook

Paleoindian fishing, in this case far upriver from the coast. The fishing sites are primarily riverine and suggest that salmon were present in the late Pleistocene and perhaps before.

A thousand miles south, evidence of extensive use of salmon in Indian diets on the Columbia River dates to nearly 10,000 years ago. Located at the Roadcut site located near The Dalles, thousands of salmon bones were uncovered a few decades ago. Ensuing debate questioned whether humans were engaged in a subsistence fishery at the site, but in more recent studies, new excavations and analyses support the evidence for salmon fishing on the Columbia.

Prior to the discovery of such ancient sites, research indicated that tribes throughout the northeast Pacific region were dependent on hunting large mammals during the Pleistocene. The discovery of the fish bones contributes to knowledge of glacial refugia while calling into question this assumption.

Along the channel that would become the Strait of Juan de Fuca, the ice lobe reached westward 62 miles (100 km). As a rapid melting began over 13,000 years ago and salmon took advantage of the retreat, fishing became increasingly important to the indigenous peoples, but when that shift occurred is unknown, although humans most likely occupied the land as it rebounded from its icy burden.

Thus, as a resource for many tribes throughout the Pacific Northwest, it is evident that even with the natural ups-and-downs of yearly runs, the Chinook had a consistent, long-term presence dating to the waning years of the last glacial advance.

Beginning in the nineteenth century, all of that would change.

Fishing — Business

More than a thousand miles south of Puget Sound, by 1850 Chinook commercial fishing had begun in the Sacramento and San Joaquin rivers of central California. With the first cannery in place by 1864, twenty-two years later the closures began. Canneries were now built in more northly locations, positioned to process the rich bounty of Pacific Northwest salmon.

In Washington, the first state hatchery had been built on the Columbia River in 1891, initiating a period of intensive fishing. Such an exploitation raised social and political issues, but in time, as fishing expanded upriver, the resource — salmon — inevitably declined.

To the north, the first cannery in Puget Sound was constructed at Mukilteo in 1877, and by the beginning of the 20th century, demand was high and increasing. There, in the cold, salty waters of the Sound Chinook numbers are estimated to have been as high as 690,000, most of them natural origin fish.

The pace picked up, with the heyday of commercial Chinook fishing in the Sound commencing in the early 1980s. It continued for a decade; during that time, the harvest exceeded 200,000 fish per year. By 1994, the run was larger; estimated at 240,000 fish, the harvest included a higher percentage of hatchery fish, produced in response to declining natural origin salmon populations.

Following that maximum, Chinook numbers fell sharply, and with it the harvest: the annual count now numbered 49,000 fish. What should have served as a blaring signal of a new reality may have been heeded by some, but exploitation rates of the dwindling population remained high. The Chinook was now in free fall throughout its range.

This survivor of an oscillating climate that had honed its adaptability and expanded its range even as humans thrived on its abundance, within a few years — a mere fraction of its family's existence — the Chinook had become the object of unprecedented pressures. And although the decline was evident by the end of the nineteenth century, exploitation as the 20th century advanced created pressure on all salmon species. Radical change throughout the region, brought on by an increased human population, overwhelmed the Chinook, sending it into a staggering decline throughout its ancient home.

By the second decade of the 21st century, after listing the Puget Sound Chinook as Threatened, the commercial harvest numbered about 78,000 per year. However, by this time hatchery production dominated, and thus the natural origin take was only 3,050; the numbers declined proportionately in the recreational fishery. This low count reveals how deeply exploited the Chinook had become.

The cold reality of over 150 years of salmon fishing, both commercial and recreational, is that the natural origin Chinook population has declined from at least hundreds of thousands to the hundreds.

Given that there are many impacts on the species, including natural events and increased predator pressure throughout the region, it must be emphasized that the most precipitous drop occurred when fishing pressure intensified. Within a brief span of time, Chinook populations declined so dramatically that ultimately it was no surprise that the possibility — the reality — of listing the Puget Sound Chinook Evolutionarily Significant Unit (ESU) was necessary to save the dwindling fish. It is unfortunate that 25 years later the dream of restoration lies in the future, if it is possible to achieve it at all.

Historically, however, fishing was only one culprit in the Chinook's demise.

Habitat Loss

Fishing alone did not bring about the decline of all salmon species. On the Columbia River, the building of several dams created fish blockage on a grand scale. To the north, the construction of two dams on the Elwha River also led to the demise of many salmon populations, while other rivers underwent less dramatic but nevertheless unprecedented changes. It progressed rapidly, this legacy of human activities. River courses were straightened, banks riprapped, wood removed from streambeds, riparian forests cut, and waterways polluted from agricultural runoff, while private and commercial structures on the shores of rivers and saltwater bodies altered the shoreline, seemingly without limit. It was a time of opportunity, with an ensuing change at a magnitude few could have foreseen.

Meanwhile, the fish were subjected to a double whammy. Fished in increasing numbers from fresh waters and salt alike, the remaining salmon relentlessly swam to their natal homes that were losing the capacity to sustain them. Ultimately, natural origin Chinook Salmon would decline and, although the numbers varied across this species' range, the overall impact was essentially the same.

Listing the Puget Sound Chinook would force a new reality on planners, researchers, and the public alike. It was, in a sense, a check of how close this ESU was to extirpation. To restore it, or at least stop the decline, involved addressing issues of overfishing, habitat loss, and increased hatchery production. At the same time, the impacts of climate change on ocean productivity, competition for resources, and increased predation, would prove even more difficult to assess.

Addressing factors that could be managed, at least to some extent, it seemed that the only answer was going backward, if return to a more fish-friendly state could be called that.

Fishing of natural origin fish would have to be restricted, more than in the past. Hatchery production would have to fall under the scrutiny of citizens and scientists alike: it could not be assumed that increasing hatchery production meant restoration of natural runs.

Perhaps most difficult of all, turning back the clock on destructive shoreline practices would have to be addressed.

Structures were in place, impacts on water quality well-known, stream and river alterations a reality.

One approach would include removing land from development through acquisition and conservation designation. However, withholding properties from development was not sufficient, as alterations were pervasive. Habitat restoration, a method that considered the entire system, water and land alike, had to take on an importance previously untested.

Fortunately, there was a precedent for turning back the clock, one that could provide guidance. In the late 20th century, as the reality of the Puget Sound Chinook Salmon decline was being addressed at the highest level, restoration was already an approach being used for natural origin salmon. Such practices included altering river dynamics, a large-scale approach that, once again, was a step "back" to a pre-development state. Streamside work included enhancing riparian zones with plantings of native shrubs and trees. Short term salmon supplementation projects could restore lost populations, while increased monitoring contributed to evaluating project success.

With listing, restoration would be expanded, as more funds became available and public involvement increased. These efforts consisted of both small scale and large approaches. However, assessing the results posed new challenges — impatience for measurable impacts would have to be acknowledged, while continued commitment was an absolute necessity.

Fishing Until Listing

In 1973, the United States Congress passed the Endangered Species Act (ESA), arguably the most important environmental legislation ever written. Both reactive and visionary, this law offered a hope of halting the decline of animals and plants across the continent with ramifications for the planet itself. Clarified, revised, argued, challenged — just a few of a whole plethora of issues that would accompany the implementation and application of the ESA — since its enactment, this law has been invoked many times for the protection of salmon populations. Grouped as Evolutionarily Significant Units (ESUs), in the case of the Chinook Salmon, nine ESUs were eventually listed, two of them as Endangered and seven as Threatened throughout the species' range. In the Pacific Northwest, on May 24, 1999, three Chinook ESUs in Washington and Oregon were designated as Threatened and one as Endangered. The Threatened populations included the Puget Sound ESU, a unit that encompassed Puget Sound and Hood Canal Chinook, as well as populations north to the Canadian border, and west along the Strait to the Elwha River.

Such a listing set into motion the creation of several documents: amongst these, as required by the ESA, a Recovery Management Plan (RMP) was first published in 2005. Although lacking enforcement authority, this document provides management and research guidelines for the listed Puget Sound Chinook Salmon ESU. Target numbers are specified, as are restoration plans and fishing impact concerns, among others.

Another important document researched and written following listing was the Comprehensive Management Plan, a five-year guide written in collaboration by Puget Sound Indian Tribes and the Washington Department of Fish and Wildlife (WDFW). Among other topics, this plan specifies numbers such as the permitted exploitation rates and lists target values for the Puget Sound Chinook populations.

The National Oceanic and Atmospheric Administration (NOAA) also makes reports available to the public; one such is the periodic 5-year review.

All proposed actions and informative reports have a simple goal — the eventual delisting of the ESU. This is the ultimate intent for all ESA-listed species.

But with Chinook Salmon runs numbering in the low hundreds, and target values in the thousands, it is difficult to envision how such ideals can be reached. Thus, for the Puget Sound Chinook, more than 20 years after listing, the goal remains elusive. The directive is in place, plans and reports are written, and restoration is ongoing. Yet recovery is not evident.

Such low numbers would seem to imply that natural origin Puget Sound Chinook should not be subjected to fishing. However, this is a misconception: listing a salmon ESU as Threatened does not mean a halt to the take. Although hatchery fish are marked, thus enabling separation, an increase in hatchery fishing invariably results in a larger natural origin take as well. Thus, after listing, as the total catch increased once again, with numbers topping 100,000 by 2002, peaking at nearly 125,000 by 2007, and remaining high, it included natural origin fish. Except for poor years, such as those following the "Blob" in 2012, this *take has been higher than before listing*: this reality reflects in part this increase in hatchery-supported fisheries.

With Chinook Salmon runs in the low hundreds and targets that reflect a past perhaps not repeatable, it is difficult to project how delisting can be achieved. Unfortunately, not only are recovery sustainability figures high, but little progress has been made since listing over 20 years ago. And the expansion of hatchery production, while providing opportunities for anglers and commercial enterprises alike, does not contribute to the recovery of natural origin fish. In fact, as recently as the second decade of the 21st century, lawsuits have been filed challenging hatchery practices, particularly the taking of ESA-listed fish as hatchery broodstock. Yet augmentation with pen-hatched fish has been increasingly considered the answer to the question of restoring listed salmon.

Restoration — The Big and the Small

In 2023, the waters of the Dungeness River crept across land historically cut off from the river's ancient flow. The creation of beneficial estuarine conditions marked the culmination of years of planning and construction work, a process that involved many players, including local agencies, tribes, and conservation organizations. Begun in 2015, the Clallam County levee setback project began, with land modifications that included removal of a dike system built in the 1960s by the Army Corps of Engineers.

While restoration of the Dungeness to its ancient floodplain was the project goal, these alterations did not imply a complete reversal. The dikes that constrained the lower river would be removed, but another levee, built farther from the riverbank, was an accommodation to current realities. Private land was protected by this approach, but land acquisition for a new levee was also a necessity. This reality posed a roadblock for the entire project.

When the Jamestown S'Klallam Tribe acquired 65 acres for the levee site the restoration dream was rekindled. Completed in 2021, this structure connected with the new Clallam County levee, setting the stage for the re-entry of the Dungeness River. The river could once again spread across 143 acres of its altered floodplain.

The restoration story was not yet complete, as revegetation projects began. In 2022, the Tribe announced the intention to plant 35,000 native plants on 56 acres of tribal land. Named the River's Edge Revegetation Project, the hope is to create a riparian forest with benefits that include cooling the water, stabilizing the land, thus slowing riverbank erosion, while providing beneficial animal habitat.

A visit to the restored Dungeness River floodplain provides the opportunity to observe a mixture of past and present, as the river now spreads unfettered across much of its old course. Full of hope for permanent residents of this wetland-like habitat, for those that pass through, such as the Chinook, the expanded riverbed provides a place for rest at the beginning or end of their lives. Yet much also depends on what transpires away from the estuary, where the spawning fish seek their natal home, and the migrating fry hunt and grow.

Oncorhynchus tshawytscha - Chinook

Smaller in scale, projects upriver from the Dungeness River mouth may be less visible to the public but are important for habitat restoration. As with estuarine plantings downriver, such efforts involve riparian placement of thousands of native shrubs and trees. Beneficial impacts include riverside shading that ameliorates rising water temperature. Erosion control is also enhanced and habitat for a myriad of creatures restored. In time, a mature forest will also contribute woody debris to the river. Equally important, newly carved side channels within the new riparian habitat project reduce the rapid flow within the main river while increasing protection for salmon.

West of the Dungeness, the Elwha River is designated as the Puget Sound Chinook ESU boundary: from this point the Chinook populations are considered part of the Washington Coast Chinook ESU, a region that includes the western Strait and coastal waters as far south as the Columbia River. This ESU is under review for listing, as similar fishing exploitation and habitat alterations have resulted in a sharp declines of natural origin Chinook.

Several rivers discharge into the Strait along this stretch, most of them much smaller than the eastern rivers. A hatchery on the Hoko River, the largest of these western flows, supplements a natural Chinook population that numbers in the hundreds. The regulatory goal for the total run is 1,258 fish. The Hoko Chinook is not considered overfished.

Degradation of habitat along the Hoko has provided impetus for restoration projects, some of them large scale. A logging access road near the river is one such site; erosion has historically produced fine sediment, degrading spawning beds. Beginning in 2012, alterations included culvert removal, placement of woody debris in the river, and bridge replacement at a river crossing that previously created a barrier to the upper Hoko. A half-million-dollar project, the non-monetary return for this effort is revealed by salmon recolonization upstream of the site.

Circled Life

Most of the old growth coniferous forest along the Hoko River is gone, replaced by managed tree farms. Alongside and within the river, the implications of this historical reality are both subtle and profound. Attempts to restore the river to a healthier state — that is, a waterway that benefits from the protection and contribution of the forest — are continuing. In the 21st century, one such project augments restoration efforts that began in the early 1990s along the Little Hoko River. Proposals such as large-scale plantings near the Hoko estuary would also represent a continuation of that legacy.

Culvert removal, such as that undertaken on the upper Hoko River, represents one of the most important restorative approaches on rivers across the state. These pipes were most often built with little regard for impact on migrating fish populations. The "drop" from such structures was typically measured in feet, implying total blockage to upstream movement of spawning salmon. Other, more directly visible impacts included culvert failure, typically during storms, resulting in washed-out roads and the dumping of sediments by the tons into rivers and streams.

The requirement for increased effort in culvert removal was ordered by the Ninth Circuit court in 2016 and affirmed by the U.S. Supreme Court in 2018. The plaintiffs' claim was that culvert replacement would not only promote the return of salmon but provide mitigation against climate change impacts, such as increasingly heavy rainfall.

With millions of dollars available to fund removal projects, a drive along Highway 101 reveals the implications of the court's orders. Specific project information is posted on large signs, including the cost. Observed above the old culvert sites, returning salmon are one of the rewards.

Always poised for the opportunity to stray into newly opened habitats, the Chinook offers hope that it is not too late to save them. This is most evident on the Elwha River, a much-altered waterway with the largest "culverts" of all. The removal of two dams constructed in the early 20th century has provided an unprecedented opportunity to monitor the return of all salmon species to the river.

However, it has not been a linear path, nor should that be expected. The fluctuation of Chinook numbers in the Elwha following dam removal have driven home such realities. Hopeful numbers in the earliest years have been followed by declines and subsequent slow growth once again. Fishing the Chinook remains closed as this largest of all salmon continues its tenuous recovery.

The many facets of habitat restoration within and along river boundaries includes many diverse activities, a reflection of the complexity of a natural system much altered by human impacts. Perhaps it is more instructive that this is our reality. There is not a simple fix, and thus plantings, installation of woody structures, culvert removal, streambed alterations, land conservation, and more, all play their role. In part, because the approach is so multi-faceted, it enforces the idea of long-term commitment to the outcome of mostly short-term projects. It is a world of social and political realities, iideas new and old, and always that desire for something that is in the realm of the magical, the quick and the spectacular.

Unfortunately, there are no guarantees. Obligation and watchfulness, accountability, and science — all and more must play their roles.

Today, in the third decade of the 21st century, delisting of the Puget Sound Chinook Salmon remains an elusive goal. Progress is achingly slow, with numbers inching upwards only to undergo fluctuations once again. Nevertheless, it is fortunate for these mighty fish that restoration programs and protection from exploitation are in place. Otherwise, extinction seems inevitable.

But is it possible that listing under the Endangered Species Act is not being correctly applied? It seems that fish populations must be on the brink before petitions are submitted and addressed. Numbers are startingly low: in the case of the Puget Sound Chinook, they had cascaded from the hundreds of thousands into the hundreds. The pattern has been hauntingly repeated. Intensive fishing, unchecked development, a free fall in numbers, and then, finally, a listing is granted.

Meanwhile, before the wheels of government grind into their tardy start, citizens implement changes, hoping to create an environment in which the salmon can at the very least stabilize. Lessons from the past serve as guidelines while efforts in the present continue to instruct. And on occasion, inspiration comes from the sight of a salmon, returned from the sea to a welcoming home.

Oncorhynchus kisutch - Coho

*The tiny salmon fry scope out miniscule territories, feeding
on small insects and larvae, while aggressively defending their
patch. Born a few weeks after their parents' autumn return to
their natal stream, now once again the days shorten. Yet for the
youngsters, there seems little rush to swim seaward. Sustained
by nutritious prey, many will delay their freshwater departure
one more winter. Then, colored in new hues and patterns, the six-
inch fish — the "smolts" — move downstream with the springtime
flow, relinquishing the security of their birth home for the
engulfing sea. It is a lure they cannot resist.*

Also called the Silver Salmon, the name "Coho" is of
unknown origin although it is most likely indigenous.
Oncorhynchus means "hooked snout," and the genus includes 16
species, most of them native to the northern Pacific, ranging from
Asian waters to North America. *Kisutch* is the Russian vernacular
for the fish, a name dating back to 1792. *Oncorhynchus* species are
members of the Salmonidae family, a medium-sized group of
about 66 species which also includes graylings, whitefishes, and
others. However, in the Pacific Northwest salmon are the most
well-known of the Salmonidae, particularly for their importance
to coastal tribes for thousands of years, and, in more recent times
as a seemingly unlimited resource for commercial and
recreational fisheries.

The Coho is the third largest of the native Pacific salmon; both
the great Chinook and the less well-known Chum are heavier and
longer. Coho can reach a maximum length of about 38.5 inches (97
cm) and a weight of nearly 31 pounds, but more commonly they
tip the scales at 6 to 12 pounds, with the larger males
approximately 28 inches (71 cm) in length and the female 23.5
inches (59.5 cm). In other words, this is a two-foot fish weighing
in like a medium-size bag of flour.

During their years of maturation in the ocean, Coho are
silvery on the sides, bluish gray above, with a white belly. They

have small black spots above the lateral line and on the upper lobe of the caudal fin. The lining of the mouth is white, the body elongated, and the upper jaw extends beyond the eye. The body scales are large and sparse. This classic, beautiful fish is closely related to Chinook Salmon.

Coho are anadromous, returning in autumn to their natal stream to spawn and die, most often after one winter at sea. Factors such as increased river flow and high tides promote upstream movement. Occasionally, younger, smaller fish, known as "jacks," spawn less than a year after their saltwater residency and survive to migrate back to the ocean, only to return upriver once again. Coho fry may spend two winters in their birthplace, eventually moving downstream towards estuaries where they undergo the physiological changes necessary for adaptation to saltwater. The adults are known to travel farther upstream than most other species, spawning in shallow waters of narrow creeks, or sometimes in larger rivers as well.

***Oncorhynchus kisutch* - Coho Salmon**

Oncorhynchus kisutch - Coho

Wide ranging, the Coho is distributed from the Bering Sea to
Monterey Bay, California, and across the Pacific to northern Japan
and eastern Russia, including the Kamchatka Peninsula and the
Sea of Okhotsk. Coho have also been introduced to the Great
Lakes and other locations long distances from their Pacific home
and are raised in fish farms and hatcheries alike. In the Salish Sea,
they are present in all large rivers and many streams. Although
historically numbering in the hundreds of thousands, today the
Coho is the second least abundant salmon species, not including
sea-run trout such as Cutthroat.

During their ocean residency, Coho typically remain near the
continental shelf, migrating shorter distances than other salmon
species. If they do leave the local waters, fish that enter the ocean
via the Strait probably move northward.

When Coho begin their homeward journey, they must
undergo a "reverse" adaptation, this time from saltwater to fresh.
Such a change coincides with a transformation from their oceanic
silvery color to warm hues, and the development of the male's
hooked upper jaw and enlarged teeth. At this time, the males are
deep red, resembling a Chinook salmon, and are accented with
bands on the sides; females are more bronze in color with a paler
dorsal surface. Both sexes retain their spots. Strong swimmers
against the flow, they move upstream, seeking a gravelly site
where the female digs a depression and deposits up to 3,000 eggs.
Emerging within 5-12 weeks, the juveniles remain in the substrate
for a few more weeks. Most of the young fish spend 1-4 winters in
their natal stream (northern populations tend to stay longer)
before making their way in springtime to an estuary and
eventually saltwater; there the juveniles tend to remain close to
the coast, often hidden in kelp or eelgrass.

Maturing adults eat fish and invertebrates — squid is a
particular favorite — and in turn are preyed upon by marine
mammals, larger fish, and birds. And, of course, humans.

Circled Life

Feeding Humankind — Abundance and Loss

As with other salmon species, Coho were an important food source to Indigenous peoples for countless generations. With its firm flesh, it was not only sustaining but desirable for its taste. The species was abundant; in the early years of commercial fishing, the catch in the Columbia River alone numbered 900,000 fish. By the 1930s, in part due to the construction of dams, that bounty was consigned to memory and, until a growth in hatchery production, the catch remained low. Hatcheries built specifically for augmenting the declining natural origin (also called "wild") Coho population had been constructed as early as the late 19th century. On the Elwha River, dams built in the early 20th century reduced salmon runs, including the Coho, to the merest shadow of their former abundance. In response, in 1976 the Lower Elwha Klallam Tribe built a hatchery on the river to increase the Coho population.

In the past, the Coho supported fisheries in California, but with sharp declines beginning in the mid-20th century, by the early 1990s fishing this iconic species was closed throughout the state. In 1996 the Central California Coast Significant Evolutionary Unit (ESU) Coho was listed as Threatened under the Endangered Species Act (ESA). By 2005, this cohort had been relisted as Endangered. It is predicted by many that Coho will disappear from almost all California streams soon: most of these small coastal waterways have fewer than 100 wild spawning adults. In 2023, a five-year review of the endangered central California ESU noted that while some threats, such as habitat loss, had eased, other factors like climate change, were increasingly contributing to the downward trend. It seems unlikely that this small population will significantly increase; in fact, the opposite outcome is probably more likely.

Sharp reductions in wild Coho populations have not been

restricted to California. Of the seven Coho ESUs defined by the National Marine Fisheries Service (NMFS) in the three Pacific Coast states, four are listed under the ESA, including one in the lower Columbia River. In the Strait, two ESUs are defined, one west of Salt Creek (the Olympic Peninsula ESU) to the Pacific, and the other east of the creek — that population is part of the Puget Sound/Strait of Georgia ESU and is considered a "species of concern." In general, ESUs are composed of both hatchery and natural origin fish; however, for management purposes only the Dungeness and Elwha Rivers include hatchery fish. These are regulated by the Pacific Salmon Treaty between the United States and Canada.

The abundance of natural origin Coho of the past is lost in the reality of the present and the worry about the future. Bred to support fisheries in the ocean and inland waters, hatchery smolts number in the hundreds of thousands. These are fish that live along the outer coast, in rivers and streams, and in the Strait itself. As for the natural origin fish, restrictive management reflects the loss. Millions have been reduced to thousands, and in some years, those thousands are very small indeed.

2018 – The Strait's Wild Coho in Trouble

"Optimum yield (OY) means the number of fish that will provide the greatest overall benefit to the Nation, particularly with respect to food production and recreational opportunities, and taking into account protection of marine ecosystems. It is prescribed on the basis of the maximum sustainable yield (MSY) from the fishery, reduced by any relevant economic, social, or ecological factors, and provides for rebuilding of an overfished stock, taking into account the effects of uncertainty and management imprecision." – from the Pacific Coast Salmon Fishery Management Plan.

Circled Life

For the purposes of fishery management, which is the responsibility of both state and federal agencies, "overfishing" is a compilation of several factors. There is fishing, which includes commercial, tribal, and recreational harvesting of both natural origin and hatchery salmon. Other forces that contribute are predation, food availability at sea, ocean conditions, and more. For the Strait's natural origin Coho, overfishing is declared to occur if the 3-year geometric mean of spawning escapement (the number of fish that live to adulthood and return to their natal stream) falls below a specified percentage of the maximum sustainable yield (MSY): this is defined as the number of spawners that can be caught while sustaining a maximum production rate. The MSY is a particularly important concept for fisheries management; for the Strait Coho it has been estimated to be 11,000 spawning-age fish.

The percentage of this MSY that defines overfishing is specified in the Pacific Coast Salmon Fishery Management Plan (FMP). First adopted as a regulatory document for the 1977 fishing season, it was written in response to the federal Magnuson-Stevenson Act (MSA) of 1976. The plan has been modified through amendments extensively since its inception. Among other specifications, the FMP delineates the several Coho stocks of the west coast.

For the natural origin Coho, the FMP specifies the "SMSY as the number of spawners needed to produce the MSY." What its definition and use as a management tool means is that the population is believed to be sustainable indefinitely at this SMSY value; again, this number is based upon the concept of a maximum production rate. The minimum allowed threshold for spawners (MSST) is a proportion of that number. This has been set at 7,000 fish for the Strait's Coho. In other words, although the MSY, the value that sustains a maximum production rate, is calculated at 11,000, exploitation is permitted that reduces the population to 7,000 fish.

Oncorhynchus kisutch - Coho

However, If the estimated number of 3-year-old Coho (the spawning age) falls below 7,000 for three years, a Recovery Management Plan must be developed and implemented.

This is what occurred with the natural origin Coho of the Strait of Juan de Fuca in 2018. At that time, the maximum exploitation rate (ER) — that is, proportion of adult spawners that can be caught in a season — was set at 20 percent.

Prior to the recognition of the overfished Coho status in the Strait, beginning in 2014 the ocean had been anomalously warm. In part, the elevated temperature was attributed to the "Blob" that developed in the Gulf of Alaska in 2013, but other factors were unfavorable as well. The Pacific Decadal Oscillation (PDO) was also strongly positive (warmer) during this time. By 2017, the postseason estimate of the Strait natural origin Coho population was less than 5,000. And although ocean conditions had improved, indicating a possible recovery for the Coho and other species as well, the reality was an alarmingly depressed number of natural origin fish.

But before the hope for a natural recovery, what was the exploitation rate of the Strait Coho during the warm years?

In 2014, "total fishing mortality" of the Juan de Fuca (JDF) natural origin Coho was 2,327 fish; by 2016, the number was about a tenth of that value. That 2014 number represented an exploitation rate of about 18 percent of the estimated Coho population. By 2015, the return had fallen to fewer than 4,000 spawners, although preseason estimates were still above the 11,000 MSY number. The exploitation rate remained about the same, although the catch was less — the reduced Coho numbers could not sustain the allowed take. By this time, the postseason Coho estimate was fewer than 5,000 fish.

Clearly, the methods for predicting ocean abundance had failed, with the consequence that a high exploitation rate continued even as the catch numbers reflected the Coho population decline. Ultimately, the low numbers from 2015-2017 would require the implementation of a recovery plan.

This Salmon Rebuilding Plan for the "Strait of Juan de Fuca Natural Coho" salmon is a lengthy document that considers the many variables involved with recovery. Economic factors, overfishing status, regulatory specifications, environmental (habitat) considerations, and ultimately, recommendations (required for recovery), are all addressed in the plan. Finally, alternative actions are presented. In the end, "Alternative One," the status quo (or "no action) approach was selected.

In other words, the Strait of Juan de Fuca Coho were predicted to increase in number without changes to fishing regulations. In the Appendix (11) which describes this alternative, it is noteworthy (and expected) that this recovery plan would create no adverse effects on other environmental and economic considerations. This status quo alternative projected a 4-6-year recovery time frame.

Since 2019, what trends in the Strait of Juan de Fuca Coho are indicative of recovery? And what has been the escapement since the overfishing declaration? The answers are complicated.

By 2017, numbers increased to 9,374 adult spawning Coho, and the exploitation rate was 7 percent.

Meanwhile, the marine survival rate for the Strait's Coho has declined since the beginning of the 21st century. For those fish returning in 2022 the rate was 4.5 percent. Nevertheless, in 2021 the predicted escapement was 20,000 natural origin Coho in the Strait, over twice the number in 2020. And in 2024 the natural origin Coho return is estimated at more than 28,000. This encouraging number is based on a survival rate of 6.8 percent, a value that fisheries' personnel "in the field" say is optimistic. The rate is most often lower, the consequence being that many fewer spawners than predicted will return to their natal stream. And as with other salmon species the Coho varies in abundance, even in the absence of human impacts.

Oncorhynchus kisutch - Coho

Fishing seasons are set by quotas based upon annual predictions of stock size and escapement. The management principle is to permit fishing that brings the population near the maximum sustainable yield but to permit exploitation that can reduce the number below that value.

Thus, the Coho fishery permitted depends upon the accuracy of the annual population prediction.

Counting the Coho

Suppose that you knew the number of hatchery Coho smolts released into a river that terminates in the Strait. Perhaps it is a couple hundred thousand. Released from their holding ponds these fish make their way towards the saltwater, undergoing physiological changes as they swim downstream, taking advantage of new prey, and within a year or two, transforming into silvery-blue, white-bellied three-year-olds. Now mature, the adults embark upon the final stage of their lives, answering a compelling call to reproduce. And so, they begin the arduous return journey, this time from salt to freshwater, back to the river where their lives began.

As the tired fish arrive at the hatchery, you dutifully record how many have returned. Simple enough. Except, of course, somewhere in the vastness of the sea and the river, the lives of most of the smolts have been snuffed out, and even if they reach maturity, not all will succeed in the journey to the hatchery.

Not only that but the loss varies, sometimes widely, from year to year. And as a fisheries biologist, or perhaps an observer, you know many of the reasons why most smolts never become adults. You also know that understanding the causes behind varying mortality is important not only to the continuance of hatchery fish, but to the species itself.

Today, understanding the factors that can ensure successful

maturation and spawning is the responsibility of those involved with ensuring their continuance. The salmon's fate rests in human hands.

In the past, the return of spawning fish to their natal stream was also a concern for the peoples of the Strait who depended on them for life itself. The quantification of stock and the complexities of management may have been less, but expectation of the annual return was part of a cultural awareness and response that was quite different than today. Most people who fish recreationally are not dependent on their catch for survival, and even commercial fishers can look elsewhere for employment or aid if their efforts do not earn a living.

This was not the case for those who relied upon fish for survival. And it would be a mistake to think that people who depended on salmon were not aware of the ups-and-downs of fish populations. The appearance of these great fish in a freshwater stream or river was an anticipated event, acknowledged with ceremony. Present for only a few weeks, the salmon provided sustenance for an entire year.

In the 21st century, salmon fishing has long been an "industry," one regulated by local and national agencies, and subject to laws and international agreements designed to ensure species' survival. With a primary goal of providing fishing opportunities, such responsibilities are complicated and involve many employees whose actions impact millions of fish.

Part of the regulatory process for fisheries' employees involves counting these mostly unseen animals living beneath the surface of the water. Without that count, understanding the dynamics of the population is not possible.

Thus, an inventory of hatchery or natural origin Coho during the spawning season is a vital part of fisheries management. The problem is that counting is both difficult and subject to available funds, the result being that consistency is sometimes compromised, leaving many questions unanswered.

Oncorhynchus kisutch - Coho

For example, suppose historical counts provide a baseline for estimating both hatchery and natural origin returning salmon numbers. And then, for reasons not fully understood, the spawning fish count is half of what was predicted. What has transpired?

Although the annual variability in salmon dynamics complicates the work of those tasked with understanding the population complexities, such insight has become necessary. Today, research includes studying many factors, and with the availability of survey data, mathematical modeling of salmon populations has become increasingly important to managing fisheries.

What are the mortality factors that biologists attempt to quantify? To begin with, there is "natural" mortality; that is, the death rate in the absence of human predation. Difficult to predict, this rate is often treated as a constant. However, survival is in large measure determined by oceanic fluctuations; productivity depends on sometimes widely varying numbers, such as the abundance of planktonic life upon which the fish depend. This can be driven by seasonal weather fluctuations such the El Niño/La Niña cycles. The impact of temperature swings on ocean biota is difficult to quantify, but the outcome is often clear. Juvenile fish may simply starve for lack of food in warmer waters.

From the tiniest members of the food chain upon which the maturing salmon depends, to the threat of predators, including fish, birds, and marine mammals, the path to adulthood for salmon is characterized by challenges and successes alike. And, of course, there is the clever human, the most dangerous predator of all.

These challenges to survival can result in extremely high salmon mortality rates. The thousands of eggs deposited by a spawning female will for the most part fail to produce an adult.

Estimating predation by animals such as seals at sea may be

difficult, but the impact of human fishing should be more tractable. Quantifying the catch provides an estimate of population reduction and returning spawners, and such methods have been part of fishery management for many years. However, there is always the problem of incomplete counts and errors as well — these include the death of released fish, the incorrect retention of natural origin fish, and bycatch. How can such errors be quantified?

There is also the problem of stock mixing. For example, if you are fishing off the Washington coast, perhaps near the entrance to the Strait, how do you know which river a landed Coho came from? Coho do not migrate great distances, but they do move about in search of food. Thus, anglers and commercial fishers alike may catch salmon from multiple natal streams and rivers.

If, as well, you are concerned with the status and preservation of natural origin fish, what methods do you employ to ensure their separation from hatchery fish? Hatcheries exist in large part because ancient wild runs could not withstand decades of fishing pressure. And the harvest is far from your only concern; studies have demonstrated the vital importance of natural origin salmon to entire ecosystems. Thus, treating hatchery fish as a one-to-one substitute for ancient runs is an unsupportable concept.

There is an emotional, historical appeal as well, accompanied by a worrisome uncertainty about the disappearance of natural origin fish.

In addition, there are fluctuations in hatchery returns, as these fish, fed and grown in fabricated structures, are prone to problems and weaknesses associated with confinement.

So, if you are part of a fisheries' team dealing with so many unknowns, how do you improve the accuracy of predicting salmon escapement, a variable dependent on many difficult-to-quantify factors? Additionally, how do you stop the freefall of natural origin salmon, which, by law, you are required to do. And how do you distinguish these protected fish from those that are produced in hatcheries?

One answer to the last question is to mark the hatchery fish. In the 1990s, as a response to the continuing free fall in natural origin salmon populations the Washington Department of Fish and Wildlife (WDFW) began removing the adipose fin — a small projection on the back of the salmon —of Coho and Chinook hatchery fish. Thus, distinguishing these fish required a check for this small fin. If it was present, the fish would be of natural origin and therefore released. With this program the "mark-selective" fishery began, implying seasonal rules that restricted the natural origin catch to a few weeks. Along with proper management, this separation of the catch would in theory halt the decline of natural origin salmon.

A second question concerning both wild and hatchery salmon was how to separate the stocks. By doing so, the impact of fishing and other factors could be more clearly quantified. Indian treaty rights could also be more accurately addressed, and hatchery success understood in more detail. Fortunately, the development of a coded-wire tag (CWT) program, begun in the 1960s and implemented in hatchery fish in 1971, provided a means for enumerating individual fish that included recording their origins. In time, implementation of the program would result in the tagging of millions of juvenile salmon. Since its initial inception, improvements in the tags have provided increased accuracy. Although not all fish are tagged, recoveries number in the hundreds of thousands, enough for statistical analysis.

Tagging and marking programs have enabled fishery personnel to assess population dynamics for hatchery releases and unmarked natural origin fish as well. Currently, Coho salmon populations are divided into 123 groups, consisting of tagged, hatchery fish, and unmarked components. Thus, in total there are 246 Coho stocks. The number of surveyed Coho fisheries is 198, including pre-terminal and terminal; the latter refers to fisheries that are directed towards fish returning up rivers and streams.

Processing the Data with FRAM — Fishery Regulatory Assessment Model

Improvements, such as the implementation of electronic tag detection, easier-to-read tags, and faster methods for injecting the coded wire, are part of the ongoing efforts to use CWT to count returning fish and to increase knowledge of individual stock dynamics. Yet the recording of potentially thousands of numbers creates a new problem. How do you save the data for processing? Fortunately, a data repository provided by the Regional Mark Processing Center (RMIS) stores millions of numbers. As for processing that data? Computers — the ultimate (to date) high speed machine — provide the means.

Given that reduction in time and the mind-boggling work for handling thousands of entries provided by electronic computing, the question now becomes of what to do with it all. How is the data to be interpreted? What do you know about the system represented by so many numbers?

This is where modeling, in this case of fish population dynamics, offers an answer. Many systems, from airplane navigation to traffic flow, have been and are continually interpreted and improved by a modeling approach. And as with these physical systems, the dynamics of fish populations can be modeled as well. And, like an airplane where data input and the mathematical relationships between variables enables prediction of the "state," so too with fish, at least in theory. As with most other systems, however, fish dynamics are a stochastic process; that is, the factors that define the system depend on random variables, such as counting errors.

In airplane navigation, many stochastic models incorporate statistical knowledge of errors, such as sensor accuracy (for example, radar, or GPS). In the case of fish, such information may be lacking or rudimentary. Hence, a simpler approach to modeling the system is a deterministic method, where errors are specified as constants, and the data is compared to a base period, consisting of variables collected over a designated time frame.

On an airplane, you want to accurately know where you are and where you are going; for fish stocks, understanding what will transpire this year, if certain parameters are incorporated into the calculations, is the goal. The output of such a model? How many fish will escape (that is, survive the pitfalls that decrease their numbers) given the estimated starting population and the modeled impacts on that initial population estimate.

Designed in part as a response to Indian fishery rights litigation in the 1970s, FRAM (Fishery Regulation Assessment Model) is a deterministic, time-step model (five time-steps for Coho) used to evaluate proposed fisheries' impacts for a single management year. It is simplistic in concept, with user input of fishery errors (such as retaining of natural origin fish in mark-selective fisheries), and other errors as well, and, most importantly, exploitation rate. This parameter is set as a percentage, a quota, a ceiling, or as a constant.

The input of a FRAM run includes estimated stock abundances for the year as well as the fixed error values. Initial stock numbers are independently determined by fisheries biologists and include such factors as jack-to-adult relationships, smolt production, marine survival rate, and consideration of historic ocean abundance. This estimated starting value is multiplied by a constant and applies only to three-year-old Coho. FRAM calculates predicted escapement for the current year, but it can also be used "backwards" to ascertain the accuracy of this value against the actual stock assessment. This is done by using the annual Coded-wire tag (CWT) data.

The importance of FRAM is in part its use as a predictor of annual escapement, and like all models, it depends on user input. Ultimately, permitted fishing depends on that number and its relationship to the concept of maximum sustainable yield discussed above. In other words, if fish numbers are predicted to be high, so, too, is potential exploitation rate.

How well does FRAM perform? If the pre-season prediction of stock abundance is fairly accurate to begin with, then the calculated escapement also tends to come close. However, if the initial salmon stock estimate is incorrect, and especially if it is significantly above "truth," the model performs poorly.

What is most unfortunate about this discrepancy between reality and prediction is that permitted fishing can result in a high exploitation rate as the stock declines (because it is a percentage of a smaller number), meaning that there is a lag in correcting the original inaccuracy in the estimated abundance.

For example, from 2004 to 2007 when Coho populations fell dramatically, the exploitation rate was high. FRAM runs were very inaccurate, although by the following year, estimates of the Strait's Coho population were adjusted to reflect the poor year. Meanwhile, FRAM runs would be made on data that in 2008 was almost 600% over forecast. Similarly, during a subsequent crash from 2017 to 2019, one of sufficient severity that "overfished" status was declared in 2018 and a rebuilding plan implemented as required, the predicted return in 2017 had been 13,100 spawners; the actual was 4,600.

Nine years prior to this decline, in 2006 the preseason abundance was predicted at 26,100 fish; the postseason estimate 4,600. The ratio is 5.65.

The impact of incorrect forecasting of stock populations can depress stock numbers at a rapid rate, with the permitted exploitation rate eventually falling. The rebuilding plan itself acknowledges management errors in setting the fishing season from 2014 to 2015.

By using data from the current season, postseason FRAM runs provide insight into the outcome of fishery regulations and other factors, such as marine survival. It can also be used as a check on modeling assumptions and calculations, and is useful in estimating preseason abundance for the upcoming year.

Meanwhile, the optimistic 2024 prediction for the natural origin Coho in the Strait assumes a high survival rate and permits an exploitation rate of 40 percent. Encouraging as the estimate is, reporting, counting, and the passage of time will reveal the true status of the fragile Coho population.

Strait of Juan de Fuca Wild Coho – the Future

In the 21st century, sharp crashes in natural origin Coho populations in the Strait of Juan de Fuca have occurred at least twice, with the second event sufficiently severe to invoke a requirement to rebuild the stock. The fish of the eastern Strait are considered a "species of concern" in the Federal Register; however, that status is not recognized by the WDFW. In 2010, a petition to list the Coho as Endangered or Threatened in the Puget Sound region was turned down by the NMFS. And, as one of the hardest to estimate and most important impacts on Coho, marine survival is strongly influenced by ocean conditions. The cyclical nature of this factor has always been difficult to predict. The reality of climate change is equally hard to quantify. A more conservative approach might be advisable, but that does not seem likely. High exploitation rates permitted by the Fishery Management Plan depend on estimated abundance; additionally, pressure from many of those involved with the salmon fishery is always intense. Also, certain numbers, such as the maximum sustainable yield are treated as constants — they do not necessarily reflect the annual reality. Finally, fish are managed for exploitation.

Thus, the Coho and other salmon species will never be as numerous as they once were, nor is that the goal. The hope is that better knowledge of salmon dynamics will continue to boost the population. It seems that once "listed," recovery is extremely difficult.

One possible answer, if not the most desirable, to what one researcher calls "sputtering" Coho populations, is that hatchery production of Coho salmon will increase in the future. Yet with climate change and other factors as well, hatcheries also deal with declining returns that are not always well understood. The hope that hatchery fish will contribute to sustaining natural origin populations may be difficult to realize. Raised to provide fishing opportunities, hatchery fish will never be a replacement for those fish whose former abundance is consigned to memory. Has the wild Coho reached a perilous state, always on the edge?

As goes the fish, so goes the ocean. All of us are dependent on the sea, a reality that we would be wise to consider.

Oncorhynchus mykiss - Steelhead

If salmon species were to be judged for the complexity of their behavior, Steelhead would win the prize. Rather like an adolescent human in the throes of life changes, the fish often gives the impression of a calm, settled personality. Yet beneath this appearance an underlying turmoil occasionally erupts. A Steelhead might stay near its natal home for a year, or perhaps two. Then one day for unknown reasons the juvenile embarks on a seaward journey. There, the wanderer might migrate far from its birthplace, while less driven companions remain close to home, sometimes poking their noses into salty waters, other times remaining in the fresh.

The timing for a voyage home also imposes decisions on the maturing Steelhead. It might wait a year or two, growing fat on nutritious oceanic life, but eventually even the largest fish yields to the ancient call. Returning from salt water to fresh, swimming against the river's flow, losing strength as it goes, the brilliantly colored adult enters freshwater once again, there to search for a mate amongst the other travelers.

But rest is elusive and with its genetic legacy ensured, with a swish of its great tail, the Steelhead returns to the sea. Staying home will wait another year.

Although the origin of the common name is obscure, as one of the "hooked snout" species this *Oncorhynchus* genus member is a close relative to six other Strait of Juan de Fuca salmon species. The species' name, *mykiss,* a Russian vernacular word, hints at the wide geographical range of this complex salmon. Placed into several subspecies — *irideus* is the Steelhead subspecies in the Strait — this division suggests the variable habitats in which *Oncorhynchus mykiss* lives, places that have molded the species not only for color and size, but for its salt or freshwater preference. Most people refer to Steelhead as a trout rather than salmon, in part because the riverine form goes by the name of Rainbow Trout.

Circled Life

Yet, whatever the designation, the Steelhead is an *Oncorhynchus*, and thus a member of the Salmonidae family, but unlike most salmon, it is a species with two lifestyles. And as with its closest relatives, for thousands of years both forms provided sustenance to humans who lived near saltwater coasts and western rivers alike.

Elongated and fusiform, the adult Steelhead has a large head, a jaw that extends beyond the posterior eye margin, small teeth (at least until spawning season), large scales, and, in its sea-run form a metallic blue to bluish-green hue on top with silvery sides and white tones below. There are small black spots on the body and the dorsal and caudal fins. The maximum length is 45 inches (114 cm) with a weight of 37.9 pounds, but such large fish are uncommon; more often Steelhead adults weigh less than 10 pounds with a length of approximately 2 feet (61 cm). During spawning season, the male develops a hooked upper jaw and elongated teeth and transforms from silvery to a rosy-pink color

***Oncorhynchus mykiss* - Steelhead**

along its sides; the rest of the body is dark green.

Historically, the natural range of the Steelhead stretched across the northern Pacific from Japan, Kamchatka, and the Bering Sea to the coastal waters of the Baja Peninsula in Mexico; today the species is absent south of San Luis Obispo County in central California. Spawning populations once thrived in big and small rivers alike; the Columbia River and Snake River supported runs, and on the northern Olympic Peninsula Steelhead were plentiful in the Elwha River, the Dungeness, the Hoko, and smaller streams and rivers that empty into the Strait.

With its distinct two forms — the sea-run Steelhead and the freshwater Rainbow trout— *Oncorhynchus mykiss* is widely spread, but it is also known for its atypical spawning behavior. Unlike the truly anadromous salmon, which die after spawning, the Steelhead is an iteroparous species, meaning that both males and females sometimes survive spawning, returning downriver, where they are known as "kelts." Although this behavior is uncommon in their native range, introduced Steelhead, such as those in the Great Lakes, are often repeat spawners.

This coming-and-going can increase the lifetime of an adult Steelhead to eight years, while typically a kelt does not return to freshwater in consecutive years. In river or lake habitat, spawning adults occasionally interbreed with native rainbows, and at least one study has shown that this tendency, where present, contributes to the genetic diversity of the local population. Offspring from such mixes sometimes take up the iteroparous lifestyle, while others spend their lives in their freshwater birthplace.

Although Steelhead spawning occurs in spring, there are two distinct runs: these include the winter, composed of mature fish that spawn the following spring, and the summer run of young fish, which may spend up to a year in a river or stream before spawning.

The juveniles also exhibit a variable life history. They most often remain in their natal stream for two winters, migrating to saltwater in April or May, but occasionally departing after a single season. Young males that remain in their birthplace sometimes breed with resident trout: conversely, resident Rainbow males occasionally fertilize the eggs of returning Steelhead females.

Highly migratory Steelhead have been caught a thousand miles (1,600 km) offshore within a few months of the start of their seaward journey, while many move northward to the Aleutians or westward to Russian waters. Not all undertake such long forays, and studies indicate that juveniles from the same spawning grounds can exhibit different lifestyles in their saltwater residency. This variability is reflected in return times, as some Steelhead might remain in saltwater for only a year, while others linger for as many as three or four. It has also been observed that northern Steelhead are more likely to remain at sea for multiple seasons.

Juvenile freshwater Steelhead feed on aquatic insects, amphipods, and fish eggs. As adults the diet expands to include crustaceans, squid, and fish. In turn, seabirds find the young quite tasty, while larger predators such as lampreys, dogfish, seals, and whales, consume the mature fish.

Steelhead are closely related to the Cutthroat Trout (*Oncorhynchus clarkii*) and to an Asian species, the Cherry Salmon (*O. masou*). Their lineage has been traced to a Miocene species that lived approximately five million years ago. Named *Oncorhynchus lacustris,* in reference to its habitat in an ancient lake, such an occurrence may imply a freshwater origin for Steelhead and other salmon as well, although the topic is debated. What is known indicates that in the past, as the oceans cooled, Steelhead and other salmon species began their long tenure in the Northwest rivers that emptied into the sea. There they would mature, returning to their birthplace to spawn, and sometimes die.

Feeding the People

Like blood coursing through arteries and veins, creating and defining the life of an organism, so, too, did the salmon populate the rivers and streams of the Pacific Northwest, enriching their waters for other species. While the contributions of Steelhead yielded slowly to research, in the past this great pulse of life was appreciated by those who depended upon it. Without salmon, many human cultures could not have developed their rich complexities; fish were the staff of life for so very many.

Early European and American explorers quickly recognized the importance of salmon to indigenous diets: Lewis and Clark observed both local fishing efforts as well as the preservation of fish. The expedition benefitted from trade for these magnificent creatures, which enriched their diet and augmented provisions depleted by months spent traversing the continent. Indigenous people honored the fish with ceremony and art, while everywhere along the waterways the salmon played an integral part of life.

Steelhead was particularly important to people who lived near rivers that flow from the western Olympic mountains into the north Pacific. These included the Quinault, the Queets, the Quileute, and the Hoh. Along the Strait, Steelhead runs in the Elwha, the Dungeness, and the Hoko rivers, among other waterways, provided nourishment for local tribes.

By the late nineteenth century, Steelhead proved to be a bountiful resource as settlers began an intense commercial and recreational harvest. Unfortunately, dams severely impacted Steelhead and other salmon populations: in particular, in the early 20th century, two dams built on the Elwha reduced many species to mere fractions of their former abundance. Although historically considered the richest of the salmonid populations, with blocked access Steelhead numbers plummeted. But it was not only the Elwha where runs were reduced; Steelhead would, a hundred years later, become a remnant species. Once numbering in the millions, with stunning rapidity, the population was reduced to thousands.

Fishing the Steelhead — Commercial Bounty, Recreational Joy

Maturing from six-inch smolts tipping the scales at a few ounces, to a weight of 10 pounds, after a residency of one-to-four years, adult Steelhead return to their natal stream. With numbers unimaginable today, in Puget Sound at the beginning of the twentieth century, estimates indicated that more than 929,000 spawning adults passed through, while along the Strait, a conduit for this enormous run, thousands more turned right to thrash their way up Olympic Peninsula rivers and narrow streams alike. It was a great time to enjoy the seemingly limitless bounty. In the early years of commercial fishing there was money to be made. And for the angler, sport to be had.

Today, estimates of natural origin (also referred to as "wild") Steelhead in Puget Sound are such a shadow of the past that it is difficult to fully grasp the change in just one hundred years. On average, fisheries' personnel count approximately 14,000 adult Steelhead in Puget Sound, while rivers along the Strait support severely reduced numbers. On the Dungeness, the building of a hatchery in 1902 augmented the run, but these were captive fish, quite different in their life history and genetic robustness from the ancient populations.

Prior to the mid-20th century, separating natural origin from hatchery fish was difficult, a gap particularly significant in fisheries which caught both. Adipose fin clipping, a method to distinguish the two, was still years in the future. While this implementation would improve Steelhead estimates and inform fishing regulations, the species continued in free fall.

Throughout the heady years of unrestrained fishing, other

impacts on Steelhead contributed to their decline. Habitat loss from riverside and upstream construction, runoff alterations, logging, stream course straightening, degradation of water quality, and many other human endeavors were factors in the Steelhead loss. And although natural origin fish are robust, they are also quite specific in their requirements. Particularly for spawning.

Although not considered the tastiest salmon, by the end of the nineteenth century Steelhead would nevertheless occupy an important role in cannery production. In part, the species filled the vacancy left by the declining Chinook salmon. Canneries popped up like mushrooms, particularly along the Columbia River. Here, the river served as conduit for exporting millions of cans around the world. Frozen fish were also popular in the international market.

It was exploitation on a massive scale, and it could not last. Unfortunately, this was a time of inconsistent record keeping, but if the fish were gone, so, too, was the industry. The last cannery along the Columbia River did not close until 1980, but as early as the 1920s the steady decline had begun. From its status as a regular family food item, salmon, including Steelhead, became a restaurant specialty, while in time recreational fishing began to equal the commercial take.

Meanwhile, along the coast and the Strait, as with many other salmon populations, local Steelhead went into a decline of their own. It was relentless, and ultimately the specter of extinction began to hang over many runs. Based on historic records, Olympic coastal populations are estimated to have declined by 55% since 1950. In the Elwha, of course, except for the Rainbow Trout form, the species was essentially gone, while in the Dungeness the record was poor as well, reflecting both overfishing and loss of habitat throughout the Salish Sea.

Circled Life

Hatcheries – the "Answer" That Will Not Die

Today, fish hatcheries are under scrutiny for their efforts towards salmon restoration. The stated primary goal of these facilities is to ensure the survival of natural origin populations, but throughout history the reality has been their role in supporting fishing, including recreational, commercial, and subsistence. Certainly, maintaining historic fish runs is less lucrative and difficult to quantify. Eventually, the system of hatcheries in Washington would become the largest in the world, with approximately 200 million juvenile fish raised in more than 100 state, federal, and tribal facilities.

With the goal of supporting the natural origin runs by taking pressure off them (even the most ardent advocate of hatchery-raised fish probably does not equate these fish with wild ones), in the early years, hatcheries must have seemed like the answer. And the exploitation of salmon, including the Steelhead, is evident from how quickly hatchery construction proceeded. The first was authorized in 1891 and built in 1895. From 1900-1945 alone, Steelhead production in the Dungeness hatchery numbered nearly two million. Such a high count supported the best fishery in the state.

In the Strait, hoping to restore salmon runs, the Lower Elwha Klallam tribe built a hatchery on the Elwha River in 1975. To the east, the Dungeness River hatchery continued to raise Dungeness Chinook and Coho, while downstream at Hurd Creek, Steelhead were produced annually.

Hatcheries have always seemed like an obvious answer. Yet the number of natural origin salmon continues to fall.

Fish-and-wildlife policy specifies the requirements for state-run hatcheries. However, a new guideline, C-3624, adopted in 2020, is believed by many to have weakened hatchery policy.

Oncorhynchus mykiss **- Steelhead**

Although this document states that the primary purpose of hatcheries is to ensure the continuance of natural origin salmon, including the Steelhead, "sustainable economic" benefits are also to be considered. The Washington Department of Fish and Wildlife (WDFW) must, as always, wear two hats.

That said, hatchery management and goals have changed over the many years of salmon fishing throughout the region. And directives now include consideration of habitat loss (and the possibilities for reversing and correcting the trend), tribal rights, and the preservation of listed mammals, such as the Southern Resident Orca (SRO) whale population. All are important to salmon management in the 21st century.

With general guidelines specified in documents such as C-3624, it is acknowledged by regulatory agencies that hatcheries should also be managed on an individual basis, as each embodies a different history with individual concerns and needs. Some are perhaps "state of the art," but programs and standards vary both in their modernity and effectiveness. They are not all the same.

Listing the Steelhead – the Entire Strait

Along the Strait, the natural origin Steelhead that spawn in the cold rivers and streams have declined to fractions of their former abundance. The Salt Creek winter run has been reduced by at least 43%; the Hoko decline is similar. Dams on the Elwha River nearly doomed the Steelhead there, and in the eastern Strait, Steelhead that inhabited the small streams emptying into Sequim and Discovery Bays now hang on as remnant populations. Yet compared to the coastal region the pressure was less, perhaps because of fewer numbers, or the presence of dams that effectively eliminated the species in the region.

Meanwhile, Steelhead runs in the large coastal rivers were until recent times deemed "healthy," but that status would be lost within a few years. And thus in 2022, the depressed numbers were serious enough to provoke two conservation groups into action.

Two Distinct Population Segments (DPS) are represented in the Strait of Juan de Fuca for Steelhead. A DPS is defined as a discrete population with significance to the entire species. One is the Puget Sound DPS, listed in 2007 as Threatened under the Endangered Species Act (ESA). This DPS includes the entire Puget Sound basin and the Olympic Peninsula to Salt Creek. To the west, the Olympic Peninsula DPS covers the area from the creek to Neah Bay and south to Willapa Bay.

On August 1, 2022, Wild Fish Conservancy Northwest and The Conservation Angler organizations petitioned the Secretary of Commerce for the listing of the Olympic Peninsula Steelhead DPS as a threatened or endangered population under the auspices of the ESA. Both petitioners are nonprofit groups based in Washington state. The two also requested that "critical habitat" be designated. The letter notes that the National Marine Fisheries Service (NMFS) has jurisdiction over this request.

A ruling on the petition has not yet been made, but it is interesting that such a move came after years of reports covering the ups-and-downs of the formerly great runs in the western rivers of the Olympic Peninsula. The summary notes that the summer run is nearly extinct, and the winter run is rapidly declining. The document also reveals that commercial fishing in the Pacific has continued despite sharp declines, and that in many streams and rivers hatchery fish have replaced natural origin Steelhead.

If this petition is approved, the Olympic Peninsula DPS will join a list of protected Steelhead DPSs throughout the west. In fact, of the 15 segments in the western states, 11 are Threatened or Endangered. *Since the listings began in the 1990s, none have been removed from the designation.*

One outcome of listing the Olympic Peninsula DPS would be that the entire Strait of Juan de Fuca Steelhead population would be included in recovery plans.

Listing the Steelhead — The Distinct Population Segments (DPS) Concept

It is perhaps easiest to understand the status of natural origin Steelhead throughout its historic range by considering the current EPA listing of the several DPSs, and the background of the concept. The DPS approach is primarily a means to separate a species into groups, based upon their specific habitat, range, and breeding cycle. The concept dates to the 1976 passage of the Magnuson-Stevens Fishery Conservation and Management Act, reauthorized in 2007, and its history reflects the attempts by agencies to grapple with how to define a group. A species-wide regulatory inclusion was from the start too broad a definition for legislating and managing impact: population designations cut across boundaries that were too large. And it is a reality of fish dynamics that some subset of the whole may be healthy, while others are seriously threatened.

Enacted in 1973, the ESA embodied the concept of variation within a species and the need to maintain biodiversity. Thus, at the time the DPS was seen as a valuable tool for recognizing differences that contributed to a species' health whiles requiring more protection and focusing of resources. Yet the concept was still too vague to provide clear direction, and in 1996 a new policy was developed to guide designation of distinct Steelhead groups.

A DPS may be recognized without listing it, as the group must be scientifically demonstrated to be important to the survival of the species. Additionally, genetic diversity within a DPS must be considered necessary for preservation of both the species and the ecosystem.

Efforts to clarify the concept since the 1996 policy was accepted have been ongoing, with some calling for a revamping of the language that directs the specification and listing of a DPS. While the definition is altered with the goal of determining specific guidelines, listing petitions continue to be submitted. One of these is for the Olympic Peninsula Steelhead DPS.

Since the two Steelhead Distinct Population Segments of the Salish Sea and coast encompass large territories, for the purpose of state regulations, as well as local considerations of species' dynamics, the DPS units are further divided into "populations." Additionally, state regulations are applied to specific areas. For example, Sequim and Discovery Bays are part of Area 6, whereas the western Strait is included in Areas 4 and 5. Within these regions a "stock" is a specific population in a lake, river, or stream that is reproductively isolated, either by season, location, or biology.

In the Strait of Juan de Fuca, 14 Steelhead stocks are recognized; this is from a total of 60 for Puget Sound. Statewide, there are 443 defined salmonid stocks; these are periodically evaluated for their health. There are five categories – Healthy, Depressed, Critical, Unknown, and Extinct— these definitions have not changed since the original specification in 1992.

However, the methods for evaluating stock status have changed. Today, factors such as habitat, landscape use, stream conditions (woody debris, and other factors), and life history are given an importance not previously acknowledged. Definitions have changed as well; for example, the use of an "available habitat" designation has been modified. Thus, in the past a stock may have been rated "healthy" when in fact the numbers were low.

In the 21st century, more data is available than in the past for assessing the status of Steelhead stocks. Documentation such as the "Steelhead at Risk Report" considers data back to 2013 in evaluating Steelhead status throughout the state. However, given recent closures in Steelhead fisheries, it is worrisome that improvement is slow or stalled - the quest to list Olympic Peninsula Steelhead as threatened or endangered confirms this reality.

Oncorhynchus mykiss - Steelhead

To List a DPS

The ESA is specific about the criteria for listing and the definition of recovery as well. The implications for what appears to be a simple goal — delisting — can be complicated, expensive, and long term. Knowledge of a specific DPS must be advanced, threats new and historic identified, issues such as climate change studied, and the goal of harvesting considered: the list is lengthy and getting longer. Any recommendations are made within the context of the involvement of many organizations, along with consideration of population history, and the necessity of cooperation between groups with diverse interests. Success in listing a DPS is a process that requires thorough research. It is anything but automatic approval.

However, even if listing can be difficult to achieve, the criteria for delisting are specific. As stated in the Steelhead Recovery Plan for the Puget Sound DPS these are (1) Viability Criteria — the DPS will have a negligible risk of extinction over a 100-year period, and (2) Listing Factor Criteria — the NMFS will evaluate whether declines have been addressed and mitigated. More specifically, five listing factors from the ESA must be considered – (A) destruction of species' habitat or range, (B) overutilization (fishing, scientific, educational) (C) Disease or predation (D) inadequacy of regulatory mechanism, and (E) other factors that affect species' existence.

In a sense, these factors are an acknowledgement of what caused the decline of the species in question and require that those be adequately addressed. Ultimately, of course, the proof is in the numbers. Is the natural origin Steelhead of Puget Sound increasing?

Circled Life

Recovery — The Dream and the Plan

As required after listing, the NMFS was directed to create a recovery plan for the Puget Sound Steelhead. Once adopted, such a plan is not regulatory but rather a compendium of observations and recommendations. The plan was published in 2019, although the Puget Sound Steelhead DPS had been listed in 2007. Eight years later it had been noted that the decline had not stopped nor reversed.

The plan is a lengthy document (291 pages) that includes both generalities and specifics for Puget Sound Steelhead recovery. The strategies and actions are aimed at three population levels; these include the DPS, the Major Population Group (MPG,) and, at the smallest scale, the Demographically Independent Populations (DIP). The last is a population that is found in a particular lake or stream and does not interbreed with other DIPs; an example is the Elwha River Steelhead.

The goal of the plan is simplicity itself — delisting — but the emphasis is specific. The strategy for recovery is to increase "production habitats," a focus directed towards restoration of rivers and streams, within the waterways and along the banks as well.

With these ideals in mind, several strategies are specified. The plan acknowledges the steep decline of natural origin Steelhead populations and provides recovery actions that have measurable criteria. Factors which have contributed to decreasing numbers are itemized, and include impacts such as urbanization, dams, land use, and more. Of these, 10 are noted as the most significant; biological impacts, such as the interactions between hatchery and natural origin fish, as well as climate change and timber management, are amongst the ten. Each is addressed in the plan with suggestions that sometimes embody lofty goals while at the same time offering specific recommendations. Cooperation between various agencies involved with Steelhead is called for, a list that includes at least 19 entities. Coordination with plans for other listed species, such as Puget Sound Chinook is also mentioned for its importance to overall salmon restoration.

Increased monitoring is acknowledged as important while potential costs are included in the plan as well. And the necessity of detailed recovery actions is emphasized. The plan also states the importance of commitment of groups responsible for Steelhead recovery.

Elusive Recovery – The Maximum Sustained Harvest (MSH) Concept

The fishery closures occur with monotonous regularity. In the first four months of 2022, Steelhead sport fishing was halted in several Olympic coast rivers. It wasn't the coast alone, as Steelhead fishing also closed in other state rivers and streams. In 2023, more fishing opportunities were available, but Steelhead numbers are considered chronically low and less than predictions. Closures for hatchery Steelhead recognize the impact of fishing on natural origin populations.

While intended to protect natural origin Steelhead, such shutdowns result in excess hatchery fish — those that are not caught because of the early ending of a fishing season — an outcome disliked by anglers and managers alike. Thus, as controversy accompanies seasonal fishing regulation changes, the conclusion seems clear— the Steelhead remains at the brink.

In addition to the concerns over habitat degradation, interbreeding of natural origin and hatchery fish, climate change, and other factors, one notable failure is that natural origin Steelhead returns have been consistently less than predictions. This deficit not only influences decisions about fishing closures but is indicative of the difficulty in forecasting fish dynamics. Most worrisome is that the numbers continue to fall. Along the western Strait, Steelhead populations of the Hoko, the Pysht, the Clallam, and West Twin River are all in decline.

When addressing the continuing decrease in natural origin Steelhead numbers, and the impact of fishing regulations on this worrisome trend, it is important to consider how predicted "escapement" — meaning the number of fish that complete their life cycle by spawning in their natal stream — is determined. Each year the escapement goal of winter run Steelhead (summer run are not monitored) is calculated.

Today, for unlisted salmon populations the Washington Department of Fish and Wildlife relies on the Maximum Sustained Harvest (MSH) concept. As the name implies, the MSH uses an approach that aims to provide maximum harvests from a population while maintaining fish numbers at a specified level. A simplistic concept, or at least one without sufficient data to support it, setting limits with an MSH approach may contribute to the lack of success in consistently calculating escapement.

In 1985, a paper that detailed the MSH method provided guidelines for natural origin Steelhead management. The approach embodied quantifying spawner-recruit (S/R) relationships, although admittedly data was sparse. To determine input, the S/R numbers were standardized by potential juvenile parr production (PPP) as an input to a mathematical model. This parameter is the number of parr counted by various methods, such as snorkeling. Along with spawner numbers for a specific stream, the PPP is an input to the MSH model. Since long term data for PPP is not available for many river systems, assumptions are made about the application from more complete surveys to those populations lacking quantification. Data is acquired from several sources and divided into tributaries and mainstems. Only rivers that were "fully seeded," meaning supporting Steelhead at maximum production, were considered. Measurements such as habitat composition, gradient, and other parameters were taken at study sites; these included several creeks that drain into the Strait.

***Oncorhynchus mykiss* - Steelhead**

Parr density dependence on discharge rate was noted; "avoidance" was also quantified as well as preference for habitats such as riffles. Data insufficiencies such as differences between various gradient "zones" necessitating assuming parr distribution was similar between tributaries and mainstems. Application of a multiplier to the PPP, calculated by the model as .264 (26.5 spawners/1000 PPP) provided estimates of spawners needed for a specific system. This number was then used to determine the escapement goal. Thus, in the end, the model depends on the potential parr production calculation, determined by surveys, and mathematical modeling of the data.

Yet, even with all the assumptions and estimates, the incorporation of available data as an input to the mathematical model was considered to provide sufficient accuracy for its use as a management tool with further research needs specified.

Nevertheless, in 2007 the Puget Sound Steelhead was listed as threatened, and, in 2016, natural origin Steelhead fishing was prohibited throughout the Salish Sea.

With listing, jurisdiction over the Puget Sound Steelhead was transferred from state management to the National Oceanic and Atmospheric Administration (NOAA). Today, permits for incidental taking of natural origin Steelhead must be made on an individual fishery basis, and such impacts are based upon exploitation rate limits. For those Steelhead not currently listed, such as the western Strait and coastal waters, management continues with the MSH approach.

One of the problems with any management method is that with a small initial population, prediction inaccuracies can have a large impact. Annual fluctuations in productivity, sea conditions, survey efforts, mortality rates, and the competition from hatchery fish, among others, contribute to the uncertainty.

Circled Life

On the Strait - The Dungeness and the Elwha

Difficult to survey, in part because river runoff during spawning is high which makes redd (nest) counts inaccurate, the Dungeness River mixes the natural origin and the domesticated. Habitat destruction from a variety of impacts such as agriculture, dikes, and removal of woody material on the river is endemic. Hope lies in large scale improvements such as the recently concluded widening of the Dungeness flood plain near the mouth, and unprecedented construction of side channels in the river itself.

Lack of data concerning the impact of hatchery releases complicates management of the river for natural origin Steelhead protection, although it is estimated that in the past as many as 4,900 spawned in the river and its tributaries. Today, a "critical threshold" for winter Steelhead is considered to be 125 fish. Recent numbers were approximately 400, a number considerably less than the proposed recovery figure from 1,200 to 4,100. Meanwhile, concerns over the genetic introgression of hatchery fish into the Dungeness natural origin stock continue, without clear resolution.

Smaller streams such as Snow Creek reveal the ups-and-downs of natural origin Steelhead, a reality that may reflect a past of spawner fluctuations. In fact, numbers are expected to vary from year to year in any natural origin or hatchery population. In 2023, a count of 57 spawning Steelhead in Snow Creek gave encouragement for the status of the fish: as low as this number is, nevertheless it is the highest in over 20 years and slightly more than the annual average. In 2024 the smolt count also provided encouragement.

Meanwhile, on the Elwha River, where dam removal has enabled the passage of salmon upstream for the first time in one hundred years, the number of returning Steelhead has increased, from a low of 100 natural origin fish to an encouraging count of

Oncorhynchus mykiss - Steelhead

approximately 2,400 spawning adults. The ancestry of these mature Steelhead is most likely mixed: it has been confirmed that genetic diversity in the Elwha has remained high.

While quantifying Steelhead numbers may always remain a challenge, it can be hoped that the plasticity of the fish and its freshwater form, the Rainbow Trout, will contribute to its restoration in the Strait and the ocean beyond. The re-born Elwha River provides such encouragement. Perhaps one day the imperiled status of this salmon will be consigned to memory while lessons learned in management of a limited resource, as all fish are, will not be forgotten.

Small, aquarium-sized net in hand, I looked down at the little fish in the holding tank. Ready to be counted, they had no knowledge of why their downstream journey had been briefly halted. These were Coho smolts, seven-inch youngsters embarked on a voyage to the sea where they would hopefully grow fat and stout, only to return in a few years to their freshwater home. The youngsters milled about, confidently it seemed, given their temporary captive status. They seemed to know where they were going — their own personal destiny.

But they were not a uniform group. Among them a few darker, more spotted smolts revealed their presence with a dash here and there, avoiding my net. Their presence noted with elevated human voices, these were natural origin Steelhead. To the observer, the young fish represented hope for a species historically in sharp decline, but perhaps creeping away from extinction. Upstream, alterations to the creek provided an improved habitat for these youngsters, who in a few years would return from their saltwater foray as adults. As I counted the smolt, it felt like we weren't just turning back the clock, but rather looking to the future.